Castles
of the World

METRO BOOKS
New York

CONTENTS

TEXTS
Gianni Guadalupi
Gabriele Reina

EDITORIAL DIRECTOR
Valeria Manferto De Fabianis

GRAPHIC LAYOUT
Maria Cucchi

EDITORIAL COORDINATION
Elisabetta Gargagli
Marcello Libra
Novella Monti
Ambra Pelliccia
Federica Romagnoli

1 *Eilean Donan Castle in the Scottish Highlands.*

2-3 *Chenonceau, one of the Loire chateaux, in France.*

4-5 *The Alcázar in Segovia, capital of the kingdom of Castile.*

6 *Belvoir Castle in Lincolnshire, reconstructed in the 19th century.*

12-13 *A fresco from the Castello del Buon Consiglio in Trento.*

14-15 *Mosaic decorations from Jaigarh Fort, in Rajasthan.*

INTRODUCTION

There is a castle in Castile (there are many: Castile means "the land of castles") named Rocafrida, with walls of gold and fine silver merlons on the battlements, and at night it is as dazzling as the midday sun. A damsel named Rosaflorida lives there. Seven counts and three dukes from Lombardy have asked for her hand in marriage, yet she is so haughty that she disdains them all. She has fallen in love with a knight, though she has never seen him. As her dowry she offers him seven castles: seven castles in Castile.

On the island of Mongaza, seven days from Wales by sea, the giant Famongomadan, whose name alone makes one tremble, sacrifices young girls on the tallest towers of his castle, tossing their bodies in the Boiling Lake. In an unnamed donjon in the land of Brittany, a door opens to reveal a hall bedecked with flowers. In the middle is a marble table with a silver chessboard, and black and white ivory chessmen are set on the chessboard. If an errant knight sits down and moves a chessman, an invisible adversary immediately responds with another move, and if the newcomer wins the game, a door opens and ten maidens come to undress him and bathe him and perfume him before leading him to a room where a beautiful lady lies with him.

The castle of the wizard Atlas stands atop a rugged boulder, surrounded by steel tempered by the demons of hell, in a rough and uncultivated valley in the Pyrenees surrounded by crags and frightful caves. The necromancer flies around the world astride a hippogryph, the winged horse that is the offspring of a griffin and a mare, and he paralyzes all those who dare to gaze upon him by dazzling them with his magic shield. Completely concealed by the brambles that have grown around it over the centuries, a castle in France awaits the arrival of the prince whose kiss will awaken Sleeping Beauty and her

court. Beyond a dark forest somewhere, atop the tallest tower of a gloomy abode, an imprudent bride cries for help after entering the secret chamber where Bluebeard has hung the corpses of the wives that preceded her. At Zenda, the summer residence of the rulers of Ruritania, a kingdom in a happy Mittel Europa of crinoline, lace, waltzes and fox hunting, there is a dungeon where the king's doubles are imprisoned before his coronation. In the Carpathian Mountains, not far from Bistritz, a loyal servant stands by the steep path leading to the village pass. He is waiting for carriages to pass so he can offer travelers the hospitality of his master, Count Dracula, who comes out of his tomb in the crypt of the ancestral chapel to give them a worthy welcome.

Literature has dotted the world with the castles of dreams and the castle of nightmares. Yet the ones built in the real world are no less fantastic. In 15th-century Italy, Pier Maria Rossi, Count of San Secondo, was the lord of 100 castles that towered over the right bank of the Po. A passionate reader of romances of chivalry, this latter-day Lombard Orlando and unwitting precursor of Don Quixote built two beautiful castles at the far ends of his domain for his beloved, one for summer and the other for winter. The name of his Dulcinea was Bianca (*Divina Bianchina*, in the words of his court poet), and so he named the castles Torrechiara and Roccabianca, whitewashing their walls so they would gleam in the forest under the moonlight. He had their halls frescoed with the most enthralling stories of courtly love, ordering that they be painted not with dazzling colors but milky grisaille hues, so his pale lady could look at them and see her own reflection.

In 11th-century Persia, the castle of Alamut, the Eagle's Nest, rising majestically atop an inaccessible summit in the mountains circling the south bank of the Caspian, became the residence of the Old Man of the Mountain, the head of a sect of *hashishiyyin*, or users of hashish. This is the Arabic word that gave our language the term "assassin." Indeed, these men were dedicated to political murder, and they used daggers or poison to kill the victims indicated by their lord, intent on getting rid of the rulers of the Near East to rule in their stead. To convince the Assassins to commit their assigned crimes without the least hesitation, the Old Man of the Mountain had created a paradise on earth at Alamut. His candidates were drugged and led into the castle, where they found delectable food, delicious wine, and obliging maidens. When they finally fell asleep, they were brought back to their everyday world, where the dreaded castellan explained that returning to paradise was simple: they simply had to follow his orders blindly. Alamut was just one of the many fortresses held by the Assassins, forming a constellation of strongholds from Gilan to Syria, a vast Kingdom of Evil. Trusted killers would swoop down from those unassailable castles to strike sultans and viziers, Muslim princes, and crusader kings. They remained in power for two centuries, and it took the Mongol invasion to destroy them.

Rajasthan, a mosaic of feudal states in northwest India, was known as the Land of Rajas because of its plethora of kings and rulers. Their domains were as large as half of Europe – or as small as a courtyard. When an Oriental princess was abducted, the kidnapper's castle was besieged for years, and only the providential poisoning of the kidnapped girl would put an end to the war.

In 1714 in Japan of the Samurai, a petite almond-eyed siren named Ejima violated the sanctity of the harem at the castle of Edo where she was the lady of honor: she had fallen in love with the actor Shingoro. He was beheaded, not because he had accepted the lady's favors but because he had dared to wear a gown emblazoned with the three mallow leaves of Tokugawa Shogunate, which the ruler had given his beloved. A crime of lèse-majesté. These are stories of castles, castellans, and chatelaines. Stories of a world apart, enclosed by massive walls like a rocky island surrounded by a moat. It was a self-sufficient microcosm, a world devoted to autarky: the life of each castle was isolation and its fate besiegement. Like fragmentary maps of a lost country, the inventories left in archives offer us lists of the materials that were stockpiled against the inevitable: grindstones and barrels of saltpeter, cauldrons and bowls, spits and trestles, skillets

for roasting chestnuts and pots for boiling capons, faggots of wood, arrows for arbalests and bows, stones to hurl through murder holes onto attackers, and ropes for the hangman's nooses, because one of the tasks of the lord of the castle was to mete out justice, whether high or low. The rooms of the lord and his consort were the only ones with objects of any value: a bedstead with three pillows, a drape, basins, blankets, sheets, painted strongboxes with the family records, chests of clothing, and – naturally – an astonishing array of weapons, from gauntlets to sallets, gorgets, cuirasses, swords and maces, the metal arsenal of the Middle Ages, and the sturdy equipment of attack and defense.

Stratified vertically like the feudal society that had created it, the castle was strictly divided into floors for the different classes. The underground levels held not only cellars and tunnels for sorties or flight in the event of attack, but also the chthonian hell of troublemakers and outcasts, those condemned to chains as well as wealthy wayfarers abducted on the main road. After all, banditry and kidnapping for ransom were normal and profitable activities of the feudal lord. The oven, woodshed, barn, stables, henhouse, pigsty, kennels, and the falcon house – guarantor of good hunting – were set around the courtyard, as were the guardhouse with archers defending the drawbridge, the kitchen with its immense fireplace where entire tree trunks could be burned, and the enormous dining room where the castellan would sit at the head of a long table, with two immobile pages standing on each side to hold resinous torches. Next to it was the chamber of justice, where villagers and vassals were judged for their minor everyday crimes, such as poaching hares, rudeness to a page, or failure to pay their tithes. The armory, located next to it, was the most beautiful room of the castle. Here, surrounded by armor, lances, and swords set against walls covered with drapes and tapestries, the lord received feudal homage and welcomed visiting peers. This room led to the chapel, where a priest would celebrate daily Mass, at which everyone had to be present. The lord's warrior ancestors were buried here, along the walls and under the floors. These tombs were marked by slabs of marble with life-size bas-relief portraits carved according to strict rules: a helmet on the figure's head, a sword at his side, spurs on his feet, gauntlets in his hands, and the family coat of arms over his head.

The bedrooms of the noble family were located on the

second floor. They were furnished very simply, and the chatelaine's chamber was the only one with a touch of luxury: armchairs upholstered in tooled leather, painted chests with the lady's trousseau, a bookstand holding an illuminated prayer book. This was also the floor with the quarters of the little court's most important officials: the seneschal, the vintner, the baker, the falconer, the chamberlain, the squire, the muleteer, the gamekeeper, and the pages – three or four to a room, where they slept on a single enormous palliasse.

The archives, granaries, and rooms for storing the goods of the fiefdom were on the third floor. Above all this, on top of the towers, were the sentinels and guards who closely observed the world around the castle.

When he was not at war, the castellan's main occupation was hunting. His consort lived amid her ladies in her own apartment. Religious duties and the liturgical ceremonies that were part of the ecclesiastical calendar were an important part of her life. Groups of guests, relatives, friends, and wayfarers often broke up the monotony of castle life, and so there were banquets and balls, games played with cards, dice, and balls, and chess, brought back from the Orient by crusaders. Small courtyard tournaments were held, and there were quintains and fights between hens and pigs. Sometimes pilgrims arrived, rewarding their hosts with tales of their travels to faraway lands. Merchants went from castle to castle to offer their marvelous wares, and roaming jesters and troubadours brought their jests and poems and songs. At the castle, the motto was "early to bed; early to rise." Those who stayed awake to keep the fire going on long winter nights would tell stories or listen to others' tales. These stories could be true and false, read or heard, and, of course, the best ones were adventurous or frightening. They recounted events that happened in the castle or involved its denizens, described ghosts appearing in towers to expiate their sins, told of the love affairs of lords and servants alike, and revolved around love and death. For example, there is the story about Count Geoffroy de Chateaubriant, who returned from a crusade unannounced, and about how his lady fainted in fright when she saw him… as a golden-haired page furtively slipped from her chamber.

This is what castle life was like in the feudal Middle Ages, when turreted fortresses dotted the countryside from Portugal to Poland. France alone had over 20,000 castles. Colossal fortresses, entrusted to the military-religious orders

– the Templars, the Hospitallers, the Teutonic Knights – were built along the threatened borders of the kingdoms established by crusaders in the Muslim-dominated Near East. Castles controlled the Alpine, Pyrenean, and Transylvanian passes, the fords across small waterways, the course of enormous rivers like the Rhine, the Danube, the Loire, and the Po. They guarded trade routes between cities and dominated borders disputed by Christians and Moors on the Iberian Peninsula, by Normans and Celts in England, and by Teutons and Slavs, Hungarians and Wallachians, Byzantines and Turks. Castles grew wider and taller, and they were fortified. Thicker walls were built to withstand siege machinery, such as catapults that hurled stones weighing 500 or 600 pounds, flaming pots, and even carrion or the corpses of prisoners, and battering rams that shattered gates and burst through walls. There were mobile towers that were taller than the ones to be attacked, used to launch a hail of arrows, boiling oil, and fiery faggots of wood, while wreckers armed with pickaxes tried to open a breach below. We could say that besieger and besieged essentially battled on equal terms, though sooner or later a castle assaulted by an implacable enemy would fall, attacked from the outside or conquered by hunger. However, the invention of gunpowder overturned the situation, marking the end of an era and, indeed, of a civilization.

Toward the mid-15th century, cannons became the decisive weapon for conquering a castle and demolishing its walls. They were given ferocious names whose sound alone was enough to inspire dread: culverin, serpentine, aspic, which meant asp-like. They could fire scrap iron, shards, and gravel against men, and increasingly larger stone cannonballs against castle walls. In 1450, the Duke of Burgundy cast a bombard weighing nearly 20 tons that could fire a 750-pound cannonball. He already owned a 17.5-ton cannon with a gloomily poetic name: Black Margaret. Naturally, attackers had to get the cannons within firing range, but once they were set up they were deadly: a well-aimed cannonball could demolish a tower. Needless to say, the use and transportation of these giants was an extraordinarily difficult task. The enormous cannon that Mehmet II used in 1453 to breach the walls of Constantinople was drawn by 50 pairs of oxen flanked by 200 men on each side to keep the cannon balanced. Ahead of it, there were 200 diggers to widen roads and 50 carpenters to reinforce bridges. It took two months to travel the distance a man on foot could cover in two days. But when it finally reached its destination, its effect was devastating, despite the fact that it could fire no more than 7 cannonballs a day.

The cannon marked the demise of the castle as a military structure. At the same time, however, it ushered in the renaissance of these structures as noble countryside residences, during an era in which the rediscovery of classical antiquity and a love for nature led to the concept that living away from cities, surrounded by fields and woods, represented an ideal of wisdom and of mental and physical health. Villas – which initially replicated small-scale castles – became popular. Notable examples can be found in the 15th-century Medici villas around Florence. Though dotted with faux battlements, their true essence was betrayed by the windows that had replaced loopholes in order to let in plenty of light and air.

As villas took on the guise of castles, castles in turn lost their austere military appearance, casting aside their forbidding defensive stonework to acquire forms that reflected this new era. Towers became spires, bastions were turned into belvederes, moats were transformed into gardens, and the surrounding woods were converted into parks. This metamorphosis swept across Europe, but it reached its apex on the banks of the Loire, in the *douce France* of the Valois, with their queens and their royal lovers. Charles VII brought the great love of his life, Agnès Sorel, the Dame de Beauté, to the castle of Loches, with her ermines, Oriental silks, and gold brocade gowns whose trains were the longest in the kingdom – while his queen pined away in Chinon. Louis XI turned Plessis-lès-Tours into the true capital of France. His 13-year-old son, Charles VIII, had yet to set foot outside Amboise, the castle where he was born, and when he rose to the throne he had it completely renovated. He brought in the spoils from his expedition to Italy, happily surrounding himself with tapestries, paintings, sculptures, and books until the day he hit his head against a doorway and died of a concussion. Louis XII and his consort Anne of Brittany spent their lives at Blois, enjoying hunting and tournaments. Francis I returned from his short-lived conquest of Milan, bringing Leonardo da Vinci with him and hosting him at Clos Lucé. Nevertheless, art was not the only thing on his mind: he had a lover in every castle throughout the Loire Valley. Henry II gave Chenonceau to his favorite, Diane de Poitiers, who turned it into the most

beautiful residence in France. However, with the king's death, his consort Catherine de' Medici gained her revenge, forcing Diane to relinquish that marvel of the crown.

During the dark times of the Wars of Religion, the Loire châteaux reverted to their defensive functions. For the kings and their courts, they were a far safer refuge than the Louvre in the heart of fanatical Paris. The châteaux were destined to lose their royal denizens when Henry IV restored peace. Finally, with Louis XIV this mosaic of royal residences was replaced by Versailles, unique and supreme.

In the meantime, outside this enchanted valley, in the rest of Europe new fortresses were built lower to make them less vulnerable to the continuous progress made in artillery, but old castles everywhere were energetically renovated with Renaissance and baroque ornamentation, following the new fashions that spread from Italy across the continent. However, some of those proud but obsolete military structures refused to don a disguise, and some of them – abandoned – decayed and fell into ruin. Romanticism, with its obsessive admiration for an illusory image of the Middle Ages, was ultimately responsible for rediscovering and redeeming these castles, rescuing them from ruin. The quintessential architect of the revival of the faux-Gothic castle was Ludwig II, King of Bavaria, whose greatest imitator was none other than Walt Disney.

This book is not intended as an exhaustive encyclopedia but as a brief anthology of castles, an overview of their various types in different countries, offering readers a broad array. It examines castles in Europe, Asia, Africa, and America; there are authentic medieval strongholds as well as artful fakes. There are pure ones that have been brought back to their original appearance by rigorous restoration and composite ones that reflect various eras and styles. There are castles that have remained faithful to their function as noble residences, but also empty ones that have been transformed into museums. Some make ends meet as sets for films about the chivalrous days of yore, while others have become profitable ventures as hotels for well-to-do tourists. There is even a hotel that pretends to be a castle, though amid so much pretension this is hardly surprising. Above all, however, there is the spellbinding charm of this lost world. Thus, this is a catalog of extraordinary ideas for all those who build castles in the air. (G.G.)

Óbidos

PORTUGAL

According to tradition, when the Visigoths invaded and occupied the Iberian Peninsula in the 5th century, they constructed the fortress around which the village of Óbidos developed. As a source of building material, they used the Roman baths located a few miles away. Today, the baths are known as Caldas da Rainha (Queen's Baths) after a Portuguese sovereign who, at the end of the 15th century, rediscovered the therapeutic properties of these waters after observing the farmers who bathed there. Public baths were extremely popular among the Arabs, who likewise took advantage of the marvelous waters nearby when they took over the castle of Óbidos and turned it into one of the main strongholds of the Portuguese region of Estremadura. After these last invaders were driven out, with the Christian Reconquest the castle was turned into a feudal residence. It fell into ruin during the 1700s, giving this small town, whose untouched medieval appearance fascinated 19th-century travelers in search of local color, exactly the right touch of romanticism. (G.G.)

From an architectural standpoint, Óbidos is one of the most famous castles in Portugal built in the Manueline style. The fortress has a quadrilateral layout that is about 100 feet long on each side, with tall crenellated and cuspidated walls. It has lovely round towers and massive square towers on the northeast and southeast ends. There was a palace, now in ruins, in the middle of the fortress. The stronghold and surrounding village were completely enclosed by massive Moorish walls, which were repeatedly rebuilt by the Portuguese kings following the Reconquest. In fact, this fortress was a favorite among the Portuguese monarchs, who expanded and decorated it. Many of the picturesquely decorated doorways and windows are still intact. A tall guard tower was built on the west side of the curtain wall, whereas on the other side the wall is connected to the Torre do Facho. The geometric layout fully respects the classic stylistic elements of Portuguese military architecture. There is only one jarring note amid so much beauty: this is where Pedro Lopez de Ayala (1313-1403) was imprisoned and wrote *Rimado de Palacio*, his embittered vision of life and society. (G.R.)

17 bottom The Arab occupiers started with the castle and then built walls around the entire village. The walls were later enlarged and reconstructed in several stages when the Portuguese drove out the invaders and regained possession of the territory.

Sintra

PORTUGAL

Praised by Byron as "the glorious Eden" but denigrated by others as "the meeting place of madmen," Sintra, at the foot of the Sintra Mountains about 18 miles from Lisbon, was the summer residence of the Portuguese monarchs from 1493 on. This was the year that King João and Queen Leonora climbed up to a cave on top of the mountain where Our Lady had appeared and remained there for eleven days, kneeling in front of her statue. Consequently, a royal palace was built in this town, and it was enlarged and embellished by later rulers up until the 18th century. In 1503, a small convent, made entirely of wood, was built on the mountain, and in 1511 it was replaced by larger masonry structure entrusted to the Hieronymite monks. On September 30, 1743, as the feast of

the patron saint was being celebrated, lightning struck the chapel, causing a fire that destroyed most of the monastery. Ten years later, an earthquake destroyed the rest. However, the last monks did not leave until 1834, and what remained of the building became overgrown with lush vegetation.

During his travels, Ferdinand of Saxe-Coburg-Gotha, prince consort of Queen Maria II, was captivated by the romantic charm of those ruins and purchased them to transform the complex into his favorite residence. However, it took 47 years to complete the work, which was entrusted to German architect Ludwig von Eschwege and Italian set designer Demetrio Cinnatti. Castelo da Penha, or the Castle of the Rock, was not finished until 1885, the year the king died. The outcome, after nearly half a century of obsessive passion for art of all kinds and origins, was a picturesque and rather incongruous blend of styles – Arabic, Gothic, Manueline, Renaissance, and Baroque – in a maze of vaults, drawbridges, keeps, chapels, cloisters, and towers. It is an extravaganza of sculptures, paintings, tapestries, and ceramics. The castle is surrounded by an immense park with camellias, banana trees, hydrangeas,

18-19 The vibrant and colorful palace at Sintra stands out against the windswept sky of Estremadura like a fairy-tale castle. Not surprisingly, this picturesque palace was designed by a scenery painter and an architect.

18 bottom Massive counterforts crowned by little towers and featuring enormous Gothic arches

sustain the foundation of part of the palace, which Prince Consort Ferdinand of Saxe-Coburg-Gotha built as his favorite residence.

19 The main entrance charmingly takes up the Manueline style, with lively ashlar work, coats of arms, and, on the sides, two slender watchtowers with semicircular segmented roofs.

firs, and geraniums form hedges so thick that even daylight cannot penetrate them. The park extends between two mountains and includes the ruins of another castle, the Moorish Castle, built by the Arab conquerors in the 8th century. The latter castle has a magnificent ring of crenellated walls rising along a hillside, with a panorama that extends to the sea. (G.G.)

The extraordinary Palacio da Penha, with its bright colors (dark gray walls, yellow minarets, and crimson towers) and capricious forms, is located on the northern side of the granite mountain after which the palace was named, not far from the castle built by the Moors in the 8th century. It was designed by architect Ludwig von Eschwege, who traveled to Great Britain, Germany, and Switzerland for inspiration in designing the castle. The work lasted from 1839 to 1885. The chapel of the old convent was maintained and embellished with numerous works of art. Above all, a splendid cloister in the Manueline style (an extravagant blend of Gothic, *mudejar* and *plateresco* styles that became popular in the late 15th century) was maintained, too. Each decorative element of the complex is cloaked in mystical or magical symbolism. As a result, the interior seems to span everything from Ancient Egypt to Moroccan culture, and on to the Gothic, Baroque, Manueline, and Art Deco styles, with a rich array of priceless furnishings. A majestic staircase leads to the noble hall, where plaster molded into roses and plants decorates the walls and ceiling. There is also a famous neo-Gothic chandelier made of gilded bronze and bearing 72 candles. In 1995 Sintra and the peaks of Serra de Sintra were inscribed in UNESCO's World Heritage List. (G.R.)

Sintra

20 *This frowning Atlas strains under seemingly desperate - but unwarranted - effort: the enormous window he supports has so much lacy openwork that it cannot be much of a burden for him.*

21 *top Several of the castle's decorative details copy parts of other Portuguese buildings.*

This window is an exact replica of a 16th-century window at the Convento do Cristo in Tomar.

21 *bottom Slate gray, yellow, and crimson characterize the various buildings of Castelo da Penha, or the Castle of the Rock, which took nearly 50 years to build. This work came to an end with the death of its patron.*

22 top One of the rooms at the Royal Palace is named after the swan, the symbol of purity favored by monarchs of all eras, which was used as the main decorative motif. The photograph shows some of the detail on the 16th-century ceiling.

22 center The Hall of the Coats of Arms or of the Stags, dating back to the early 16th century, is considered the most beautiful room in the Royal Palace. It has a magnificent Persian-style octagonal dome and is tiled with 17th-century azulejos with hunting and war motifs.

22 bottom The monarchs' enormous canopy bed, with exquisitely carved columns, is set in the middle of the royal chamber, which is decorated with elegant polychrome works.

22-23 Arabic, Gothic, Manueline, Renaissance, Baroque: in keeping with the eclectic tastes of the 19th century, all these styles are juxtaposed at Castelo da Penha. One of the most spectacular rooms is the Arabian Hall, which is full of "Moorish" furnishings.

23 bottom The kitchens are just as grand as the formal halls: these enormous vaulted rooms gleamed with impressive copper items and valuable ceramics. Still-life touches, fleshy pumpkins, and other vegetables complete the picture.

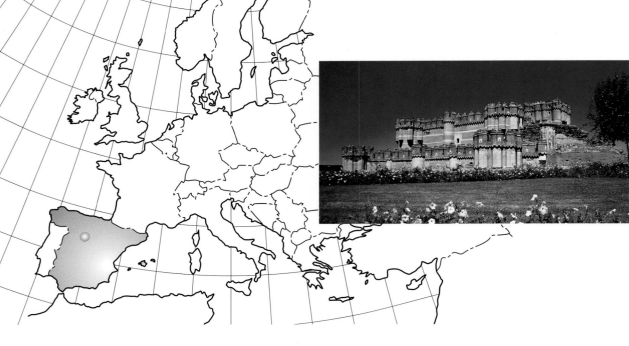

Coca

SPAIN

In about 1400, the powerful Fonseca family, the lords of Coca, had a stately castle built between Segovia and Valladolid, which was the favorite residence of the Castilian kings at the time. Its brick walls, dotted with towers, enclosed magnificent princely apartments. Praised by architectural historians as Spain's most artistic military structure, the castle unfortunately fell into ruin and was completely stripped of its furnishings. In 1828, it lost its most beautiful and distinctive features: its *azulejos*, the ceramic tiles that completely covered the floor and walls of a patio surrounded by a double gallery of marble columns. The administrator of the assets of the Duke of Alba, the owner of the castle, decided to sell everything to make some money. As it turned out, the destruction of this masterpiece proved to be the worst of deals for the administrator. The buyer paid 40 pesetas for each column, promptly reselling them for 120 pesetas each. The castle was left in ruins until the last century, when it was finally restored and used as a forestry school. Archbishop Alonso de Fonseca, who built the castle, died in Coca in 1473 and is buried in the town church, in a splendid family chapel. (G.G.)

More of a palace than a castle, the Roman "Cauca" where Emperor Theodosius was born closely resembles Castillo de la Mota. Coca was built almost entirely of masonry and clad with thin pink bricks (the preferred materials of Muslim *alarifes*). The work of Moorish laborers, it is considered a Gothic-Mozarabic masterpiece, and it creates the surreal impression of an enchanted Moorish castle. It is a complex structure with three sets of walls built around the keep and surrounded by a very deep moat. Its *chemins de ronde*, with picturesque battlements resembling lacework, are famous. The stone loopholes, set in the brickwork, are shaped like crosses inscribed in circles, and they were designed to permit lobbing as well as direct firing. The battlements are set over an uninterrupted series of stepped murder holes, arranged in sets of two over a tower with a wide embrasure. They were ingeniously designed to mimic the shape of the stockades that were set up during attacks to protect the masonry structure. Coca was proclaimed a national monument in 1931. It now houses a forestry school as well as a museum of Romanesque woodwork. (G.R.)

24 top The rosy hue of the bricks that were used to build the castle of Coca creates a surreal appearance, augmented by its craggy Gothic-Mozarabic architecture. Historians have dubbed it "Spain's most artistic military structure."

24 bottom The masonry crowning recreates the structure of the stockades that were once used to protect fortresses. The white loopholes used by crossbowmen create a stark contrast with the brickwork.

24-25 A bird's-eye view of the castle reveals its compact but light structure, enclosed by a double curtain. Its towers are crowned with distinctive deep fluting.

25 bottom Unfortunately, nothing remains of its lavish interior. The castle - which was abandoned - was completely stripped of its furnishings over the centuries. This devastation culminated in the 19th century when the azulejo tiling of one of the patios was sold.

El Real de Manzanares

SPAIN

El Real de Manzanares, on the bank of the Manzanares River about 12 miles from Madrid, was founded in 1247. It was subsequently granted as a fiefdom to one of the great figures of the Kingdom of Castile, Don Pedro Gonzalez de Mendoza. King John II later turned the fief into an earldom and gave it to Don Iñigo Lopez de Mendoza, the first Marquis of Santillana. The marquis built the castle between 1435 and 1480, commissioning Juan Guas to design it and oversee its construction. Guas was the architect who, in 1476, built Toledo's Church of San Juan de los Reyes – an Isabelline masterpiece – for the Catholic kings, Ferdinand and Isabella. During the 16th century, Philip II initially chose El Real de Manzanares as the site of the monastery of San Lorenzo. However, he later decided that the town was too close to Madrid to offer him the peaceful retreat he desired, and he chose El Escorial. (G.G.)

According to Marcel Dieulafoy, "The northern boundary of the Mudejar style is composed of fortified castles. Old Spain was a singular blend of Gothic and Muslim art. The most glorious phase of this composite civilization was dubbed *Mozarabic* (from *mosta'rib*, or "Arabicized") when it developed in Islamic Spain and *Mudejar* (from *mudeddjan*, "permitted to remain") when it took root following the Christian Reconquest. This stronghold was built near a castle owned by the famous Mendoza family, incorporating 13th- and 14th-century ruins in the new chapel. In 1480, its well-to-do owners decided to add a splendid gallery in the Isabelline-Mudejar style – the Isabelline is characterized by an extraordinary ornamental taste combined with the forms of the late-German Gothic – and a flamboyant octagonal *Torre del Homenaje*, with spherical ashlarwork and faux murder holes. The tower became one of the most famous in Spain. This union of two worlds thus spawned the last of the Spanish palace-castles, and El Real de Manzanares is the one that most skillfully merges aesthetics and function. It is currently administered by the city of Madrid. (G.R.)

26 At El Real de Manzanares - like many Gothic-Mozarabic castles - the crowning and battlements are more decorative than functional, resembling stone lacework.

27 top and center The compact structure of the castle is lightened by the chromatic contrast of the faux stepped murder holes, extending in a band from the walls and towers, and by the ashlar work of the side towers.

27 bottom The most widely admired part of the castle is the gallery in the Isabelline-Mudejar style set around the inner courtyard. A tower covered with spherical ashlar work overlooks the courtyard.

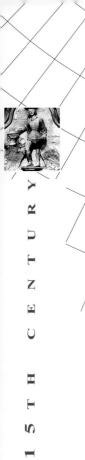

Belmonte

SPAIN

The six-towered Belmonte Castle looms starkly against the flat horizon in the heart of La Mancha, not far from Don Quixote's town of Argamasilla de Alba, El Toboso, where his beloved Dulcinea lived, and Campo de Criptana, where the Knight of the Sad Countenance capitulated before windmills he mistook for giants. Juan Fernández Pacheco, the Marquis of Villena and the all-powerful minister of Enrico IV, the King of Castile, had it built between 1456 and 1470 over the ruins of a previous fortress. It was in this castle that he later hid the monarch's daughter Juana, known as La Beltraneja, accused of being the illegitimate offspring of an adulterous relationship between her mother, Juana of Portugal, and nobleman Don Beltrán de la Cueva.

Most of the Castilian nobility refused to accept Juana as the legitimate heir to the throne and rebelled against the dishonored king, who finally declared his other daughter Isabella his heir.

During the most turbulent period of this civil war, Juana – unconvinced of Villena's loyalty – fled from Belmonte upset and half-naked, and the gate through which she escaped still bears her name. (G.G.)

Built entirely of stone, Belmonte boasts the most sophisticated and uniform geometric layout of all the palace-castles of the 15th century. Only Bellver castle in Majorca, which has a round plan (rare in Spain, frequent in Portugal, in vogue in the Orient), rivals Belmonte's perfect structure. The main walls form an equilateral triangle set in a five-pointed star. Round towers with prominent Mozarabic battlements are set at the corners, and the massive *Torre del Homenaje* straddles the curtain defending the main gate. The curvature of the low outside wall follows the outline of the main body and has several round towers. Belmonte's stepped pyramidal merlons are unique and unmistakable. In the enormous residential part of the castle, the vaulted rooms overlook the triangular patio and boast carved stone fireplaces, coffered ceilings and stuccowork in the Mudejar style. In fact, the union of Christian and Moorish art became firmly entrenched during this period (for example, the *Compendio del Arte de Carpenteria*, published by Diego Lopez de Arenas in 1632, is a treatise on Oriental art). (G.R.)

28 The heraldic emblems and symbols of the ancient power of the Villena family, the lords of Belmonte and many other fortresses in 15th-century Castile, welcome visitors as they enter the castle.

28-29 Built entirely of gray stone, Belmonte castle has a triangular main section with six round towers. It is surrounded by a low exterior curtain wall with distinctive stepped pyramidal merlons.

29 bottom The triangular courtyard is surprisingly elegant, with enormous windows and arches that contrast with the stark military roughness of the outside walls, which have virtually no openings.

30-31 *Isolated on a small plateau overlooking the town, the castle of La Calahorra was one of Spain's first Renaissance structures. It was built by Rodrigo de Mendoza, the illegitimate son of Cardinal Mendoza, the archbishop of Toledo.*

30 *bottom and* 31 *The geometric simplicity of the exterior, with its enormous towers typical of Spanish castles, conceals the exuberant richness of the interior, which has carved doorways and balustrades made of Carrara marble.*

La Calahorra
SPAIN

The little mining village of La Calahorra, located on the road from Granada to the port of Almeria, near Guadix at the foot of the Sierra Nevada, conceals one of Spain's most exquisite Renaissance structures. This is the castle built in 1510 by Rodrigo de Mendoza, the first Marquis of Zenete, for his fiefdom.

Mendoza was the illegitimate son of the great Cardinal Mendoza, the Archbishop of Toledo who went to great lengths to bring Isabella of Castile to the throne. His father granted him the estate of Zenete and the queen made him a marquis. In turn, he showed the queen his gratitude through his brilliant conduct during the Granada War that drove the Moors from Spain. He then went to Italy, where he was

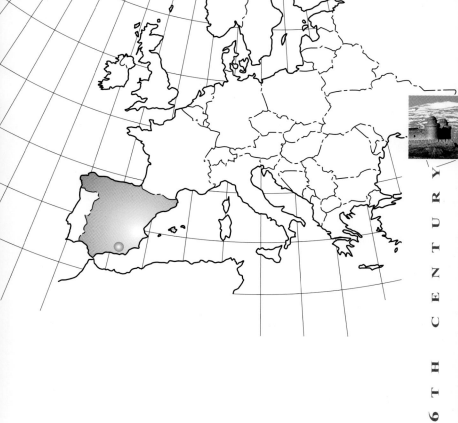

welcomed in Rome by his father's close friend Pope Alexander VI, who suggested that Rodrigo marry his daughter Lucrezia Borgia. People promptly began to ridicule the marriage between a cardinal's son and a pope's daughter: the wedding never took place and Rodrigo returned to Spain. In the meantime, however, he had fallen in love with the Renaissance artwork that was changing the face of Italian cities, and brought Genoese architect Michele Carlone back to Spain with him. He commissioned Carlone to build him a castle near La Calahorra, but he had no way of knowing that neither he nor his descendants would ever set foot in that isolated spot.

Carlone created a masterpiece for the pope's son-in-law *manqué*. Though the exterior is typical of a 15th-century Spanish fortress, with massive walls and enormous corner towers, the interior is a palace in the purest Renaissance style, with exquisitely carved doorways and balustrades made of Carrara marble. La Calahorra was the first example of the new Renaissance style, and it is rivaled only by Vélez Bianco Castle, built by a Spanish architect during the same period for the Marquis de los Vélez. (G.G.)

La Calahorra was built in 1509-1512 over a previous Muslim fortress. It is extremely important from an artistic and architectural standpoint, as it is emblematic of the transition from medieval tenets to the Renaissance style. And yet none of this is evident from the exterior. The curtain walls are tall and imposing, with rare triads of windows on each side that undoubtedly did little to illuminate the interior. The most striking features are the four corner towers. Large and cylindrical, they had scarps around the base and were topped by half-towers with hemispherical domes (a rarity in Castilian architecture), evoking the watchtowers of later centuries. The towers mute the harsh appearance of the fortress and give this complex, reddened by the dust from the Alquife mines, an aura of somber elegance. The interior is a completely different world, with an ornate Renaissance courtyard adorned with double arches and pillars, coffered ceilings, candelabras, Latin inscriptions, coats of arms, and a Carrara marble staircase with carved figures, a novelty in Spain. The decorative motifs feature the grotesques and mythological subjects distinctive of the early Renaissance. (G.R.)

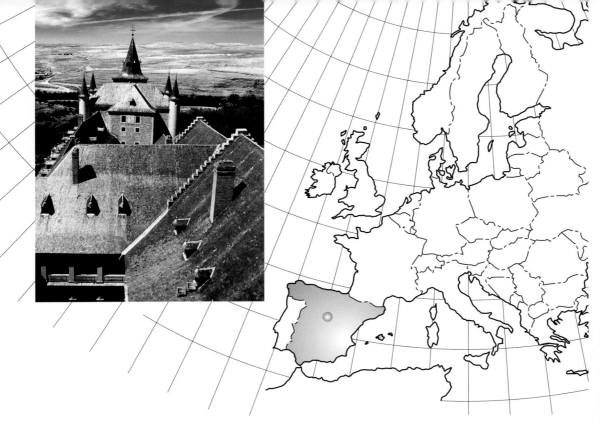

33 top right The internal
courtyard is enclosed by the tall
walls of the various wings of the
building, made of yellowish stone,
with simple rectangular windows or
more elegant Gothic doublet-lancet
windows, as seen on the right.

The Alcázar
of Segovia
SPAIN

32 Like the prow of an enormous
ship pointed towards the plains of
old Castile, the Alcázar in Segovia
rises to a height of 263 feet on a
rocky spur at the end of the city.

32-33 Segovia's Alcázar, one of
the richest and most impressive
royal residences in Spain, was built
by King Alfonso VI towards the
end of the 11th century. He wanted
an urban fortress that would rival
the Arabian stronghold in Toledo,
which had made a deep impression
on him.

33 top left The northeast entrance
is dominated by a massive
rectangular keep built in the 15th
century, which is crowned by
jutting towers and flanked by other
towers with distinctive conical
roofs.

Segovia, one of the most fascinating cities of Old Castile, is
picturesquely located on a broad rocky plateau wedged
between two streams. It was important as far back as the Roman
era (according to legend, it was founded by Hercules), and later
became the capital of an Arab kingdom and the residence of
several Castilian monarchs. Toward the end of the 11th century,
one of these rulers, Alfonso VI, built the Alcázar (from the
Arabic al-Qasr, in turn derived from the Latin word castrum, fort)
near the western end of the city, at the confluence of the Rio
Eresma and the Rio Clamores. Before he finally succeeded to the
throne, Alfonso had been driven from Castile by his brother
Sancho the Strong, who had taken over the kingdom. Alfonso
thus sought refuge with the Moors, who still occupied more
than half of the Iberian Peninsula. He took advantage of his exile
to study the position and construction of fortresses in Toledo
and other Muslim cities. When he returned to his homeland and
ascended the throne, he had a large urban castle built in
Segovia, which was very close to the border between the
Muslim and Christian territories.

The Alcázar was enlarged during the 13th century and
completely remodeled between 1352 and 1358. Part of it was
renovated under the Catholic kings and then again under
Charles V and Philip II. Philip also had the south façade rebuilt
by his favorite architect, Juan de Herrera. The castle apartments,
decorated with mosaics and frescoes, were famous. The
enormous Monarchs' Room had 52 life-size painted wooden
statues of the rulers of the ancient Spanish kingdoms of Oviedo,
Leon, and Castile, from Pelayo to Joan the Mad, who died in
1555. All this artwork was lost in a terrible fire in 1862, when
the building was occupied by the Artillery Academy. (G.G.)

The layout of this royal castle is bounded by the edge of the rocky plateau on which it was built. The entire complex is surrounded by round towers with pointed conical roofs, a feature rarely seen in Spanish architecture. The entrance to the castle is marked by a barbican that is dominated by the imposing Tower of Juan II, which is topped by semicircular turrets similar to the ones at Peñafiel, La Mota, and Coca. Just beyond this is the Patio de Armas, or courtyard. The magnificent rooms (the Pine-cone Room, the King's Chamber, the Galley Room, the Throne Room) set around the courtyard are dazzling examples of the Gothic and Mozarabic styles. In the 14th, 15th and even the 16th centuries, Spanish Christians continued to turn to Muslim masters for the construction of magnificent buildings. These rooms are also connected to the body of the Torre del Homenaje. Most of the castle was reconstructed following a fire in 1862. The Alcázar now houses a weapons museum. (G.R.)

The Alcázar of Segovia

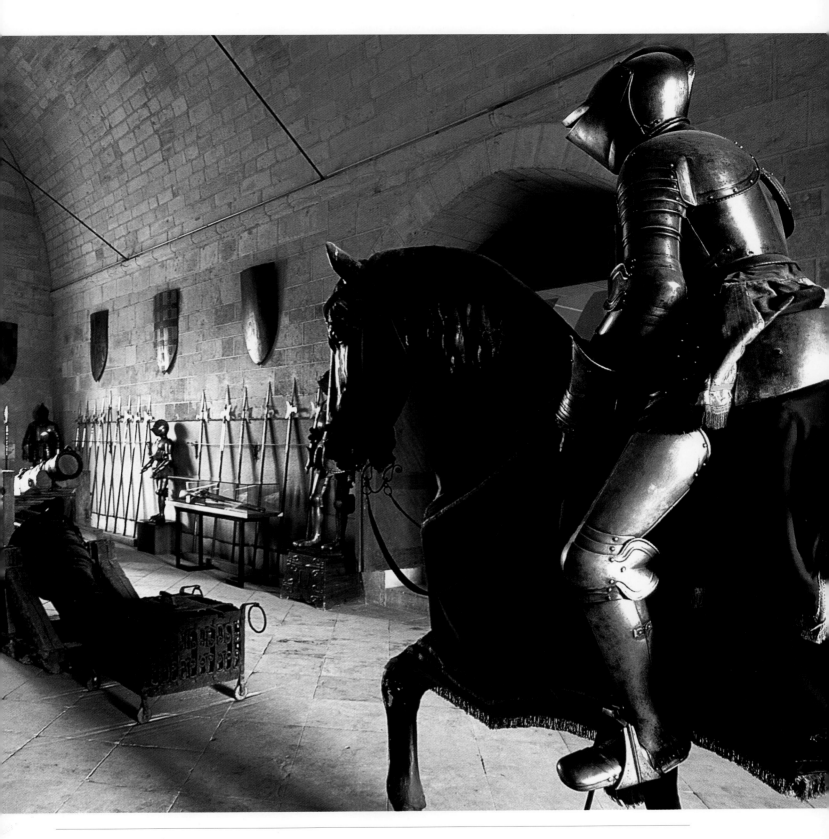

34 top Unfortunately, a fire that broke out in 1862 destroyed most of the furnishings and the decorations in this magnificent building, which was extensively renovated. The picture shows some of the detailing of the gilded dome in the Throne Room, done in the Mudejar style.

34 center Statues of the rulers of Oviedo, Leon, and Castile line the upper wall in the Sala de Juntas de los Reyes de Castilla. Christopher Columbus was supposedly received here by Ferdinand and Isabella after returning from one of his voyages to America.

34 bottom Priceless figured tapestries and 16th-century armor frame the Gothic arch leading into the Throne Room. The two royal thrones, set on a platform with the coat of arms of the Kingdom of Spain, are visible in the background.

34-35 The weapons rooms features swords, lances, pikes, halberds, cannons, and armor from the 15th-16th centuries, some of which were made by the most important armorers of the era.

The Alcázar of Segovia

36 The monarchs of Castile and Leon are portrayed on a series of windows. Here we see Henry IV - known as Henry the Impotent - whose reign was tormented by the insubordination of the great feudatories, who scorned him as weak and contemptible.

37 top Henry II, known as El De Las Mercedes and portrayed here between John I and Henry I, rose to the throne in 1369 after killing his brother Peter I (Peter the Cruel), one of the most brutal rulers in the history of Spain.

37 bottom This glass decoration from the Sala de las Pinas portrays Alfonso VIII, King of Castile and Leon, on horseback. His daughter Berenguela, born from his marriage to Eleanor of the Plantagenet family, is depicted on the left, looking down from a balcony.

38-39 The elevated position of the Alcázar gives its multiform buildings a dream-like appearance. The complex stands opposite the equally impressive and irregular architecture of the cathedral, on the left.

40-41 The château of Blois forms an incomplete square set around a large courtyard of honor. The castle is composed of four separate parts built in different periods, from the end of the 15th century to the mid-17th century.

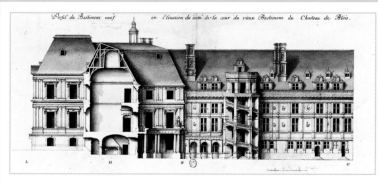

40 bottom The wing with the famous staircase of Francis I, shown here in a 16th-century drawing, is considered the loveliest part of the château. Even today, there is debate over who designed the château, French architect Jacques Sourdeau or Italian Domenico da Cortona.

Blois

FRANCE

It is likely that, as far back as the Roman era, a fortress crowned the spur dominating the Loire on one side and, on the other, one of the numerous valleys opening up along the course of the river. However, the castle did not become important until the feudal period under the counts of Blois, and later the Châtillon family. Louis, Duke of Orléans, purchased it in 1391. The ambitious second son of King Charles V was assassinated in Paris in 1407 by the minions of his cousin, the duke of Burgundy. His widow, Valentina Visconti, the daughter of Gian Galeazzo, the Duke of Milan, retreated to the castle, where she closed herself up in a room done completely in black. Overcome with grief, she died there a little more than a year later. Their son Charles, who was captured by the English during the Battle of Agincourt (1415), did not see the castle again for 25 years. During his imprisonment in England, he wrote some of the most beautiful poetry of that century. When he returned to France, the 50-year-old nobleman fell in love with 14-year-old Marie of Cleves. He married her and brought her to live at Blois, which was completely renovated and became an architectural treasure that attracted artists and men of letters.

41 bottom Henry III had the Duke of Guise and his brother, the Cardinal of Lorraine, murdered at Blois. The two were the heads of the Catholic league that threatened to depose him. The painting depicts the courtiers in an animated discussion as they stand over the body of the murdered duke.

41 top King Louis XII, portrayed in this equestrian statue in a Gothic niche over the entrance to the castle, was born in Blois. He stayed here for extended periods of time and added the wing bearing his name, Saint-Calais Chapel, and the gardens.

42 top *The private chamber of Queen Catherine de Medici boasts 237 wooden panels, inlaid with pure gold, which conceal secret storerooms. An enormous arched window brightly illuminates the chamber, located in the wing of Francis I.*

42-43 *The majestic spiral staircase of Francis I is set in an octagonal tower. Climbing balconies on the sides follow the movement of the internal spiral and are embellished with delicately sculpted arabesques.*

43 top and center The Salle des Etats - 90 feet long, 59 feet wide, and 39 feet tall - has lovely windows painted with the symbols of the monarchs. Above, the hedgehog, the emblem of Louis XII. The ermine was the emblem of Anne of Brittany, wife of Louis XII.

43 bottom The wide, low steps of the spiral staircase built by Francis I could even be climbed on horseback. Fanciful as this may seem to us today, these low steps were used for this purpose in many noble residences of the period.

Blois

At Blois, Marie gave birth to a son – the future King Louis XII – who far preferred the castle to life in Paris. His successor Francis I, who married Louis' daughter Claude, spent most of his time at Blois. However, when his young consort died in 1524, he preferred to stay at other castles, above all Chambord and Fontainebleau. Nevertheless, like his predecessors he too enlarged and renovated Blois. Henry II, Francis' son and husband of Catherine de' Medici, lived here for many years, as did their children Charles IX and Henry III, during the Wars of Religion between the Catholics and the Huguenots that devastated France and made ultra-Catholic Paris an unappealing place for these rulers to live. In fact, though they were Catholic, they made every effort to rise above the fray. It was at Blois that Henry III had the Duke of Guise and his brother, the Cardinal of Lorraine, murdered, as they were the heads of the Catholic League that threatened to depose him. The duke had been warned, but he considered the king a coward who would never have dared such a bold move. When the duke arrived at the castle, he was stabbed to death by the members of the royal guard. A few days later, as the Queen Mother Catherine de' Medici lay dying in another room at Blois, she told her son to "stitch back together after cutting out." However, Henry never had the chance to follow his mother's advice, for a short time later he too fell under the vengeful dagger of a Catholic friar.

Blois was abandoned following Henry III's death. Henry of Navarre – who was named the heir to the throne and had celebrated his betrothal to Margaret, the sister of Henry III, at the castle – went there rarely, as did his son Louis XIII, who instead used it as the gilded prison for his mother Marie de' Medici, on the advice of Cardinal Richelieu. Despite the proverbial corpulence of this illustrious prisoner, in 1619 – after being held there for two years – she managed to escape by letting herself down the wall using a rope ladder. Blois was subsequently chosen as a summer residence by the king's brother, Gaston d'Orléans, a scheming prince who set up an alternative court to the king's. The prince had Charles' apartment and part of the wing of Francis I demolished to make room for the ambitious plans drawn up by François Mansart, but only part of this work was completed. Following Gaston's death in 1660, Blois was practically abandoned. It was used as army barracks in the 19th century and was then restored between 1843 and 1870. Though this work took up the exaggerated decorative forms typical of the era (which were later removed), it saved the castle from ruin. (G.G.)

44 *The wing of Francis I features an array of Renaissance furnishings, like the canopy bed with slender posts, and the carved cabinet, tapestries, and paintings.*

44-45 *The magnificent wing of Francis I boasts enormous fireplaces, like this sculpted masterpiece that, alone, is grand enough to furnish this room.*

Blois

Paleolithic settlements testify to the extraordinary position of Blois. The earliest documentation about the castle dates back to the 9th century, when it was the fief of the counts of Blois who, up to the 13th century, attempted to rebuild the stronghold several times. Toward the end of the 15th century, enormous windows, loggias, and dormers were added to the castle, despite its quintessentially Gothic layout. Several buildings were constructed under Francis I. These masterpieces of the early French Renaissance have slate roofs with tall chimney pots, impressive skylights, balustrades with openwork, Italianate cornices, windows girded by

pilasters, and horizontal molding: these elements became the leading architectural order for all the castles of the Loire. The most famous element is the spiral staircase set in an octagonal tower jutting out into the courtyard of honor; the king and his retinue would stand at its triple balconies to welcome guests. Henry IV loved this castle and had a 655-foot portico constructed around the garden. Gaston d'Orléans had François Mansart add a wing, which was built in the classic style and clashed with the Renaissance buildings Gaston hoped to demolish. It was abandoned during the 18th century and its gardens were divided into lots. (G.R.)

45 top *The Salle des Etats, an immense vaulted hall with polychrome columns, was grandly designed to accommodate the meetings of the three "states" representing the Parliament of the Kingdom of France: the aristocracy, the clergy, and the bourgeoisie.*

46-47 In 1519, Francis I began
work to reconstruct the châteaux
of Chambord, formerly the
hunting lodge of the Counts of
Blois. He spent the last years of
his life here, despite the fact that
the colossal residence had not been
completed yet.

Chambord

FRANCE

What is now the most extraordinary of the Loire châteaux, with its forest of pinnacles and towers, 440 rooms, 60 staircases, 365 fireplaces, and acre after acre of parkland, was a modest hunting lodge owned by the counts of Blois when King Francis I purchased it in 1519 and decided to reconstruct it. It took 15 years and the toil of 1800 workmen to complete the central portion alone; the wings were added later. As far as the plans are concerned, some have cited Leonardo da Vinci, although there is no proof of this. Indeed, no one knows the name of the architect who designed Chambord, and the castle was probably the result of the brilliant work of a group of Frenchmen and Italians who joined forces to make the monarch's dream come true.

Francis I chose this spot as his favorite residence because he was a passionate hunter and had also fallen in love with the Countess of Thoury, who stayed at a château nearby. This is where the king welcomed Emperor Charles V, and it is also where he spent the last years of his life. His son, Henry II, continued the work but he too did not live to see it completed. He went there often, attracted by the plentiful game in the surrounding forests. Henry would go there with his consort, Catherine de' Medici, who would spend the day hunting with her husband and then climb to the rooftop with her astrologers in the evening to gaze at the stars and interpret the future of the kingdom. Under Louis XIII and Louis XIV, Chambord became a hunting lodge once again, but the Sun King also held memorable events at the château. He had some of Molière's comedies performed here, such as *Le Bourgeois Gentilhomme*, which was staged in 1670.

In the 18th century, Chambord hosted King Stanislas of Poland, who had been dethroned and driven out of his country, and the Marshal of Saxony, who revived the splendor of Francis I, bringing in his own cohort. Napoleon installed a court of the

46 bottom The fairy-tale appearance of the rooftops of Chambord, with its multitude of spires, chimneys, and pointed roofs, clearly stands out in this drawing from the Recueil de dessins by Androuet du Cerceau, conserved at the Musée Condé of Chantilly.

47 top It seems that Francis I, here in a portrait by Jean Clouet exhibited at the Louvre, chose this spot as his residence because of the plentiful game in the surrounding forest, but also because the beautiful Countess of Thoury lived in a château nearby.

47 bottom Emerging from the translucent airy background, Chambord stands out against the horizon in this work by Martin Pierre Denis, which depicts the château in about 1722, during a hunting match organized by the Duke of Orléans, on horseback in the foreground.

16TH
CENTURY

48-49 The simplicity of this
building, a square central body
with round towers and enormous
rectangular windows, is countered
by the unbridled profusion of
elements that make the roof a
veritable architectural jungle.

49 The side towers, topped by a
cusped roof with a lantern, are
crowned by large windows and by
chimneys that have no practical
function and are essentially
decorative.

Legion of Honor there, and then he donated it to Marshal Berthier, whose widow was forced to sell it in 1821, as she could not afford its daunting upkeep. It was purchased through a national subscription to donate it to the newborn Duke of Bordeaux, the "miracle child" born posthumously to the Duke of Berry, who had been assassinated by a fanatic. After the fall of the Bourbons, the French government attempted to confiscate the château, but a 20-year trial finally recognized the duke's rights. Upon his death in 1883 the House of Bourbon-Parma inherited Chambord. Since this noble family served in the Austro-Hungarian army during the Great War, the French government exercised its right of preemption and took over Chambord at the end of yet another seemingly endless trial among its heirs. (G.G.)

Francis I (1519), who was so infatuated with the Italian Renaissance that he dismantled an ancient fortress, can be credited with the "arabesque" appearance of the château: the "woman with the wind in her hair" evoked by Chateaubriand. The influence of Leonardo da Vinci is evident, and there are clearly ties to the wooden model made by Domenico da Cortona during the period of Charles VIII, with a square-based donjon and cruciform rooms dividing each floor into four

50 top Furnished with period furniture, Amiens tapestries, prized carpets, and canopy beds, the rooms at Chambord have maintained the aura of the château's golden age. The photograph shows a corner of the Reading Room.

50 bottom Louis XIV used Chambord as a hunting lodge and held lavish parties there. This was his ceremonial bedroom, built in 1681 and redecorated in 1748 using panels taken from Versailles.

Chambord

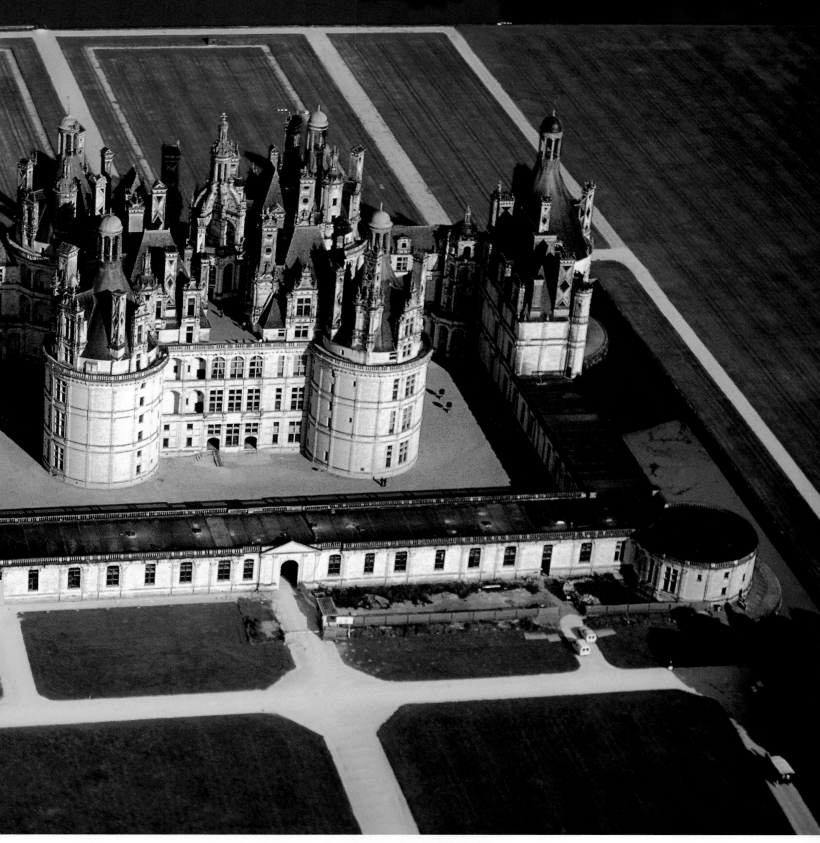

50-51 This aerial view fully reveals the fantastic labyrinth of pinnacles, towers, and chimneypots that inspired Chateaubriand to compare the château to "a woman with the wind in her hair."

51 bottom At Chambord - as at Blois - Francis I wanted a grand double circular staircase. It is 26 feet wide and the vault over it features carved coffering.

52 top left The château's most valuable furnishings include an extraordinary series of tapestries. This one, made in the 17th century by Amiens craftsmen based on cartoons by Simon Vouet, depicts Odysseus landing on the Island of Calypso.

Chambord

52 top right Odysseus, finally back at Ithaca, is recognized by his dog Argo in this tapestry from Amiens, also based on Simon Vouet's cartoons.

sectors. The work on Chambord continued until about 1547 and the château was laid out so that the donjon, the seat of the king's court, was between the wing of Francis I and the Italianate chapel, symbolically between the monarch and God. The heavy cylindrical towers, tapering upward with roofs and chimney pots that almost look out of proportion, are all that remain of the medieval structure. The entire upper part of the château is dotted with dormers with classical Italianate superstructures, pavilions, little towers, and small pediments. The broad terraces are Leonardesque, and the king's retinue would go there for a stroll or for a quiet place to sit and observe the landscape and the hunt. Above all, however, it is the double spiral staircase supported by eight square pillars, set at the intersection of four halls forming a cross and connecting the various floors of the château, that profoundly reflects the influence of the Italian master. The division of the floors into separate but identical apartments replicates the layout of the Medici villas, and the coffered ceilings reflect a classical style. Nearly all of the 440 rooms had fireplaces, but all the toilets were on the ground floor. (G.R.)

52-53 King Francis I is shown in the foreground, preparing for the hunt, in this tapestry made in Paris in the late 16th century, based on cartoons by Laurent Guyot.

53 Following the Restoration, the château of Chambord was purchased through a national subscription to donate it to the newborn Duke of Bordeaux, the grandson of King Charles X. The old monarch stayed there several times: this is his billiards room.

Chenonceau

FRANCE

The most spectacular of the Loire châteaux, built on a five-arch bridge across the Cher River, has an all-female history. In 1515, Thomas Bohier, the fabulously wealthy finance minister of Normandy, built a square castle in the early-French-Renaissance style over the foundations of a fortified mill. However, his wife Catherine Briçonnet was the one who actually oversaw the work on the château, which was still incomplete when Bohier died in Italy in 1523. Louise of Savoy, the mother of King Francis I, had the partly finished building confiscated from Bohier's son Antoine to reimburse the crown for his father's financial misdeeds. As soon as he rose to the throne in 1547, Henry II gave the château to his lover Diane de Poitiers, who hired architect Philibert Delorme to design the arches over the river. However, the king died in 1559 and his wife Catherine de' Medici finally gained the upper hand over her rival. As soon as she became regent of France, all-powerful and thirsting for revenge, she forced Diane to leave Chenonceau and had Delorme complete the gallery above the arches, holding dazzling parties and banquets that cost the state treasury a small fortune. Catherine left the château to her daughter-in-law Louise of Lorraine, the wife of Henry III, who was murdered in 1589. Louise locked herself up in Chenonceau. She always dressed in white (the royal color of mourning), living in a room done completely in black and decorated with silver funerary emblems – skulls, tears, bones, and gravediggers' spades – and constantly reciting the rosary for her husband's soul. She died in 1601 and the château went to the Vendôme and the Condé families. However, its new owners virtually abandoned the château until 1730, when it was taken over by financier Claude Dupin. He and his wife restored this marvelous structure, receiving the elite of Paris society there.

54 Because of its location straddling the Cher River, the château of Chenonceau is considered one of the finest Renaissance residences of the Loire Valley.

54-55 King Henry I gave the unfinished castle as a gift to his lover Diane de Poitiers, who hired architect Philibert Delorme to design the arches over the river. However, when the king died, Diane was forced to return the château to the queen.

55 top The rigid geometry of the Renaissance garden goes perfectly with the stark white château, which was started in 1515 by finance minister Thomas Bohier. However, Bohier died in 1523 before the work was finished.

56-57 Bohier's château (left) was built over the foundations of a fortified mill, with four round towers along the sides. Diane de Poitiers decided to add a long gallery set on five arches straddling the river.

The lovely Madame Dupin was a charming and witty hostess, and Jean-Jacques Rousseau, hired as her tutor, fell hopelessly – but unrequitedly – in love with her.

Upon her husband's death, the widow moved to Chenonceau permanently. She enjoyed such widespread esteem that during the Reign of Terror the Jacobins allowed her to live peacefully in her home, where she died in 1799 at the age of 93. It was subsequently held by a number of different owners and even today, Chenonceau is privately owned. (G.G.)

With its unique structure spanning the Cher River, this spectacular château could easily be mistaken for a covered bridge. It was constructed by Delorme, who built a highly unusual two-story wing whose façades feature cleverly designed foreparts with 18 windows and nine dormers on each side. The upper floor was magnificently decorated and used as a ballroom. Today the rooms are still

58 bottom left The salamander and the ermine, the favorite emblems of Francis I, decorate the fireplace in the enormous great hall of Louis XIV. Francis I would stay at the Bohier château when he went hunting in the region.

58 bottom right After Catherine de Medici took Chenonceau away from her rival Diane de Poitiers, she completed the gallery and held lavish parties and banquets there. This was her bedroom.

59 top The portrait of Catherine de Medici, framed by the marvelous carved fireplace, stares down at visitors. The queen, who became the regent of France after her husband's death, turned Chenonceau into her favorite residence.

58-59 Various members of the French royal family lived at Chenonceau. This room, which has an enormous fireplace, belonged to César of Vendôme, the son of King Henry IV and his lover Gabrielle d'Estrées.

59 bottom Catherine de Medici hosted parties for hundreds of guests, costing the treasury enormous sums of money, but these fêtes were part of the regent's political and diplomatic duties. A veritable army of chefs prepared exquisite dishes in these immense kitchens.

Chenonceau

60 *Diane de Poitiers in all her splendor: this painting by Francesco Primaticcio portrays the beautiful lover of Henry II as Diana the huntress, surrounded by charming cupids.*

splendidly furnished, particularly the rooms of Catherine de' Medici, César of Vendôme, Gabrielle d'Estrées, and Louis XIV, which boast paintings by Primaticcio, Nattier, Van Loo, Rigaud, and Rubens, Flemish tapestries, and monumental fireplaces by Jean Goujon. There is a small wax museum on the premises, illustrating scenes from everyday life at Chenonceau. The gardens of Diane de Poitiers and Catherine de' Medici are across from the château. (G.R.)

61 *In the room of Diane de Poitiers, also known as the Queen's Chamber, 16th-century Flemish tapestries depict the magnificence and pleasures of courtly life. In France, the entire court would move from château to château.*

Azay-Le-Rideau

FRANCE

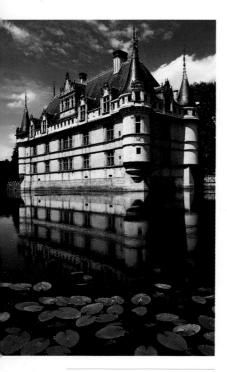

L ike Chenonceau, the château of Azay-le-Rideau – the "faceted diamond set in the Indre," as described by Balzac – was built by a successful financier. And like Chenonceau, Louise of Savoy had it confiscated from its owner, who barely escaped the gallows and fled to Flanders. The mother of Francis I was ruthless with the enormous fortunes amassed by those she called "inextricable sacrificers of France's finances." A feminine touch can also be noted in its construction: the wife of Gilles Berthelot, the fugitive, was the one who directed the work.

The Crown sold the château to bring in money, and Azay-le-Rideau was held in turn by several different owners. In the 17th century, it was purchased by Henri de Beringhen, a gentleman from the court of Louis XIII who drew the wrath of Richelieu for refusing to reveal to the terrible cardinal a secret the king had confided to him. To escape the cardinal's revenge, Beringhen went into exile in Germany. His son Jacques-Louis, who inherited Azay-le-Rideau, was also party to a sensational adventure. As he was riding to Versailles, he was kidnapped by a Dutch captain who had bet against some of his roguish friends that he could sneak into France and abduct a famous person. The victim was treated with great respect and, in turn, when his kidnappers were arrested, he hosted them at his château while "awaiting the king's orders." He presented them at court, took them to the opera and, in short, treated them with a great sense of sportsmanship. Azay-le-Rideau was sold several times after that, until finally becoming government property in 1905. Although most of its immense park was sold, the château was exquisitely restored. (G.G.)

62 top The construction of Azay-le-Rideau was supervised by the wife of the château's owner, financier Gilles Berthelot. This painting here is a portrait of one of his 18th-century descendents, Madame Marie-Henriette Berthelot de Pleneuf.

62 bottom Simple yet elegant and impressive, the façade of Azay-le-Rideau is reflected in the water of the Indre River. Part of the château is supported by piers set in the river.

62-63 *Azay-le-Rideau represents a turning point in the history of the noble residences of the Loire, marking the transition from medieval fortress to holiday home.*

63 bottom *Viewed from the air, the château - framed by greenery and ponds - truly looks like "a faceted diamond set in the Indre," according to Honoré de Balzac's eloquent description.*

64-65 In the chamber of Francis I, the ubiquitous salamander - the king's favorite emblem - stands out on the enormous fireplace.
Today the château houses a Renaissance museum.

64 bottom The portrait of Pierre Filley de la Barre, Louis XIV's marshal killed in 1705 during the Siege of Nice, is the focal point of the 17th-century blue room, so called because of the color of its décor. This was the marshal's room.

The Loire Valley was once dotted with ancient castles of which nothing is left today, and this was also the case at Azay-le-Rideau. It was replaced by a château that strove to emulate Italian architecture, built near a curve in the Indre. Piles were built to support the cream-colored tufa stone that was brought here specifically from the Cher Valley, transported on barges and carriages. Its L-shaped layout is quite unusual. The tall slate roofs are all that remain of the Gothic structure, which gained a light and graceful appearance from pediments, dormers, and scrolls and shell-shaped decorations. The façades have enormous windows and pillars with capitals supporting the cornices; an elegant row of corbels connects the four round corner towers with conical roofs. Inside, the floors are connected by a straight staircase with coffered ceilings made of stone and delimited by arches, a novelty for France's fledgling Renaissance architecture (until then, only medieval winding staircases had been used). Today the château houses the Renaissance Museum. (G.R.)

65 top The museum at the château has a vast art collection. This is a 17th-century tapestry made by Parisian craftsmen based on cartoons by Simon Vouet, illustrating an episode of Jerusalem liberated.

65 bottom Like all the castles of the Loire, Azay-le-Rideau's kitchens are enormous, brightly lit, and designed with practicality in mind, as dozens of people had to work there comfortably.

Azay-Le-Rideau

Villandry

FRANCE

66-67 Villandry is famed more for its marvelous gardens than for the building itself. The gardens were meticulously reconstructed based on the original drawings of architect Androuet du Cerceau.

66 bottom The château was constructed in 1532 by Jacques Le Breton, secretary of state for Francis I, in the pure Renaissance style that triumphantly supplanted the late Gothic in France.

67 *The courtyard of honor, surrounded on three sides by three buildings set on large arches, opens out towards the* *Cher and Loire river valleys. The building's massive foundations are completely immersed in water.*

Beautiful as the château is – a splendid example of the purest French-Renaissance style – the gardens are what give Villandry its unique charm. Its meticulously manicured square gardens have been created so that their colors change with the seasons. In its terraced gardens devoted to love, the layout of the hedges is designed to symbolize the various types of love. Boxwood hearts and flames represent "tender love," distorted hearts mean "ecstatic love," swords and daggers stand for "tragic love," and fans and letters of the alphabet symbolize "fleeting love." The reconstruction of this botanical art, which had been lost for centuries, was the work of a Spanish millionaire, Dr. Joachim Carvallo. When he purchased Villandry in 1906, he discovered the original designs of architect Androuet du Cerceau and got rid of the English park that had been planted to cover the 16th-century gardens.

The château was constructed from 1532 on by Jacques Le Breton, advisor and secretary of state for Francis I. When Le Breton purchased the land there was a medieval fortress on it, and its large square tower was incorporated in the château. In the 18th century, the last of Le Breton's descendants sold Villandry to the Marquis de Castellane, who decided to transform it "in the English style," and his son continued his work. The terraces we admire today vanished under hills and valleys, with trails winding across them and dense "picturesquely arranged" woods, as was popular among Rousseau's followers. At the same time, the façades of the château were finished with pillars and false windows to offset "unpleasant dissymmetry."

For a certain period during the Empire, the château belonged to Napoleon's eldest brother, Joseph Bonaparte, king of Spain. Following the collapse of the Napoleonic regime, Villandry was sold to the Hainguerlot family of bankers. Finally, it was purchased by Dr. Carvallo, who restored not only its original appearance but also its Renaissance spirit. (G.G.)

This elegant château was created in the 1530s by razing a feudal stronghold. The new building, with a "U" plan and L-shaped wings, boasted large cruciform windows, horizontal molding, and enormous dormers with gables and scrolls, clearly reflecting the château architecture of the Loire. Nevertheless, the fame of this residence is linked to its vast gardens. They were originally laid out as Italian-style gardens arranged on three different levels, which were modified through the limited use of Italian architectural elements, with wide paths, flowerbeds, low hedges, and decorative plants. One of the most intriguing aspects here is the use of only fruit and vegetable plants in the large colorful flowerbeds forming geometric motifs (hearts, Maltese crosses, boxwood squares, and flowers form designs symbolizing the allegories of love). (G.R.)

Villandry

69 top A complex code of amorous symbols presides over the geometric forms at the gardens at Villandry, in accordance with the precepts of 16th-century eroticism.

69 bottom The lower level of the three gardens arranged on terraces is used to grow vegetables and has nine squares divided into platbands, with different plants in a riot of colors, separated by straight paths.

68-69 Jacques Le Breton wanted to incorporate the large square tower into his new structure. The tower, shown on the left, is all that remains of the previous 14th-century feudal residence.

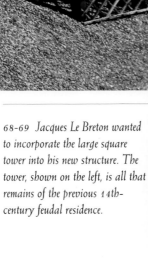

Villandry

71 top The sinuous forms of the ornamental garden of Villandry Castle guide visitors to the middle terrace, which has been defined as "boxwood embroidery."

71 bottom The hearts and flames, swords and daggers, and fans and letters of the "plant" alphabet speak their mysterious language in the flowerbeds at Villandry, designed by Androuet du Cerceau.

70-71 and 70 bottom When Spanish millionaire Carvallo purchased Villandry in 1906, he decided to restore the original design of the gardens, which had been ravaged in the early 19th century by the Marquis of Castellane. Like all 16th-century gardens, Villandry also has a boxwood maze.

Josselin

FRANCE

Brittany's most famous castle was built shortly after the year 1000 on a promontory near Ploërmel. It was constructed by a local lord, Viscount Guethenoc, who decided to name the fortress after his son Goscelin. A small town developed under its towers, as these new arrivals were attracted not only by the safety offered by the stronghold but because this was a holy place. In fact, a sanctuary marked the spot where, 200 years earlier, a farmer had found a miraculous wooden statue of Our Lady under a thorn bush. Guethenoc had the original chapel enlarged, but the pious viscount was unable to save the women in his château from the sin of pride. A poor woman came to them by the fountain where they did their laundry and begged them for something to drink, but the women of Josselin drove her away and even set their dogs after her. The roaming beggar was actually the Virgin Mary and from that day on, the women of Josselin and their descendants were condemned to howl like dogs once a year, on Pentecost Sunday.

By 1168, the fortress was powerful enough to block the army of Henry II of England, who was forced to lay long siege to it. To vent his anger, when he finally captured it he had it demolished along with its town. A few years later, Viscount Eudes II rebuilt both the town and the fortress.

In 1351, during the Breton War of Succession, one of the most famous episodes of medieval chivalry took place near the castle: the Combat of Thirty. Robert de Beaumanoir, châtelain of Josselin under the orders of the Countess of Penthièvre, and 29 of his knights challenged 30 English knights to individual combat. The English,

commanded by Richard Bembro, who occupied Ploërmel, were routed. A 19th-century obelisk still marks the field where the contest took place. During the 15th century, the castle was taken over by the de Rohan family, and various changes were made to enhance its efficiency. Finally, in 1629, Richelieu, intent on quelling the rebellious ambitions of the French nobility, had its fortifications and formidable donjon torn down. The abandoned castle was used as a prison during the French Revolution. During this period, the miraculous statue of the Virgin Mary was burnt and the sanctuary was converted into a temple of the Goddess of Reason. However, some of the faithful managed to save a fragment of the image, which is now preserved in a reliquary. The de Rohans finally restored the château in the mid-19th century. (G.G.)

72-73 Stern and impressive round towers with conical roofs crown the central portion of the castle of Josselin, built in a dazzling Gothic style. The castle was remodeled several times over the centuries and was finally restored in the 19th century.

73 bottom The castle, built on a promontory, played a key military role during the Hundred Years' War between the French and English. A famous episode in medieval chivalry - the Combat of Thirty - took place near the castle in 1351.

The old castle was destroyed and rebuilt several times. In 1491, Charles VIII of France fortuitously assisted one of its reconstructions. As compensation, he granted the de Rohan family the income from Dinan and Lehon for a five-year period so they could reconstruct their castles. As a result, Alain and Jean II de Rohan were able to restore the château magnificently, building the internal façade in pure flamboyant Gothic style – the true precursor of the Breton Renaissance – that created a stark contrast with the walls and defensive devices. In fact, on the Oust River side, the castle has a stern and rugged appearance, with an elevated body and three enormous towers rising dramatically over the riverbank. Richelieu had part of the castle demolished again during the era of Hughes de Rohan, leader of the French Huguenots. During the 17th and 18th centuries, the de Rohans resided at court, and as a result Josselin was neglected. In 1760, two towers were torn down, and in 1776, the Duchess de Rohan had a small mill installed on the ground floor. In 1835, Duke Charles-Louis began extensive renovations that revived the château's ancient splendor. The interior is of great interest; it houses valuable paintings and fine furnishings. (G.R.)

74 top Olivier de Clisson and his consort are buried near the castle, in the Basilica of Notre-Dame-du-Roncier, which once had a miraculous statue of the Virgin Mary.

74 bottom and 74-75 During the 17th and 18th centuries, Josselin was virtually abandoned by its owners, the Rohan family. Extensive restorations were finally done in about 1835, restoring the former splendor of this building, which is now lavishly furnished.

75 bottom The fireplace with the golden lilies of the royal house of France, the 18th-century globe, and the library full of exquisitely bound books can be seen at the château studio.

Haut-Koenigsbourg
FRANCE

It seems that as far back as the period of the Roman Empire there were two fortified structures on this spur jutting from the Vosges chain that dominated the Alsatian plain, with a view stretching as far as the Rhine and the Black Forest. During the 12th century, the Hohenstaufen rulers incorporated the ruins of the ancient fortresses into a new structure. In 1147, Emperor Frederick I owned one of the keeps, while the other one was held by his brother Conrad. The castle was later taken over by the Dukes of Lorraine, and in 1359 by the bishopric of Strasbourg. Its position dominated the trade routes connecting Alsace to Lorraine. During a particularly troubled period in the 15th century, it earned the dubious honor of being a refuge and base for knight-bandits, who would swoop down from the mountaintop stronghold to attack the rich caravans passing through the plains. As a result, it was captured and destroyed.

The new imperial dynasty of the Hapsburgs had it renovated and guarded by the counts of Thierstein, Sickingen and Bollwriller. Enlarged and updated to withstand the threat of the artillery, the castle was a solid sentinel on the western edge of the Holy Roman Empire until 1633, when the Swedish army captured and sacked it during the Thirty Years War. In 1648, it was taken over by the French.

76-77 Multifaceted and complex, the castle of Haut-Koenigsbourg, overlooking the Alsatian plains, was rebuilt in the early 20th century to recreate its 15th-century appearance, and it was donated to the German emperor, Wilhelm II.

Abandoned and reduced to a pile of rubble, in the 19th century it was purchased by the city of Sélestat, which gave it to Kaiser Wilhelm II of Germany in 1899, as Alsace had been taken over by the Germans in 1871. Eager to celebrate the pomp of medieval Germany, Kaiser Wilhem appointed architect Bodo Ebhardt, a restoration specialist and founder of the society for safeguarding German castles, to rebuild Haut-Koenigsbourg as it must have appeared in the 15th century. Construction, conducted with great scientific precision and a meticulous approach, lasted from 1900 to 1908. Ten years later, at the end of the Great War, Wilhelm II visited his castle for the last time. Just a few months later, the French occupied it, and President Poincaré met there with his marshals and generals to celebrate Alsace's return to France. Today Haut-Koenigsbourg is also famous among cinephiles around the world: Jean Renoir used it as the set for one of his greatest works, *Grande Illusion*, a film about World War I. (G.G.)

78 Haut-Koenigsbourg now houses a history museum with a large collection of medieval and Renaissance furnishings and items, as well as a large armory, part of which is visible in this picture.

Throughout the Middle Ages, work was done to improve and modernize the castle, particularly when the counts of Thierstein adapted it for artillery (1480-1521), studying appropriate static solutions so that the pillars, counterforts, and vaults would not be jeopardized by attacks on the external ramparts. Lovely double-lancet windows with round arches, the heavy Romanesque decorations of the square ashlared donjon, and the old *pfalz* are all that remain of the imperial Swabian stronghold made of red sandstone. France declared the ruins of the castle a national monument in 1872, and following its subsequent transfer to Germany, Bodo Ebhardt reconstructed the castle

78-79 The 15th-century main body is crowned by a massive square tower typical of German castles of this period: this was the central part of the stronghold, where the castellans lived.

based on archival documents. The castle as we see it today is the result of this work. The west side of the castle is flanked by two cylindrical keeps from the late 15th century, whose walls are up to 30 feet thick. The central body built in 1479 was also restored. It is crowned by a tall massive square tower – the *bergfried* that characterizes the architecture of German castles – and was completely rebuilt with a sloping roof. The broad bastioned façade outfitted for artillery is located on the east side, flanked by corner towers. To restore the bas-reliefs, Ebhardt commissioned sculptor Albert Kretzschlar (1832-1909), who created plaster models of all these works. A historical museum was also established, and chests, wardrobes, beds, crockery, and fabrics from the famous Lipperheide collection were brought here, as well as weapons and armor. The result is a magnificent example of fortified mountain architecture that has made Haut-Koenigsbourg one of the most visited monuments in France. (G.R.)

Haut-Koenigsbourg

80 top The side wings of Ashford castle have maintained their ancient Norman appearance, whereas the central part was remodeled in the 19th century in the style of a French château.

80 bottom The long structure, with both original and renovated Gothic windows, is covered with ivy that changes color with the seasons.

80-81 Ashford was once owned by the Guinness family, which used it as a summer home. Today it has been converted into the most luxurious hotel in Ireland, and its 83 rooms are furnished with period pieces. The castle can also be reached by sailing up the river.

Ashford Castle

IRELAND

The town of Cong, located in a magnificent natural setting between Lough Mask and Lough Corrib in County Mayo (Connaught), attracts throngs of visitors. It became famous as a typical quaint Irish village in the wake of John Ford's classic *The Quiet Man*, filmed here in 1952. However, the town's most important tourist attraction does not even appear in the movie. It is Ashford Castle, which is surrounded by an immense park and has now been transformed into the most elegant and expensive hotel in Ireland.

The Anglo-Norman de Burgo family built the castle in the 13th century when it settled in Connaught after defeating the O'Connors, who had ruled the district. Their descendants enlarged the original structure and transformed it into a sumptuous residence. In the mid-18th century, Lord Ardilaun had the central building reconstructed to resemble a French château, but did not completely eliminate the castle's original 13th-century layout. In 1852, the castle was purchased by one of Ireland's most important families, the Guinnesses, who used it as their summer residence. (G.G.)

81 top *The central portion was rebuilt by Lord Ardilaun, who purchased the building in the 18th century and asked the architect to create a faithful replica of the famous French châteaux of the Loire.*

Ashford Castle

In Ireland, the artistic features of medieval architecture are evident in ruins that have been reconstructed with a sense of aesthetics cloaked in romanticism. Ashford Castle as it appears today was built in the French style during the 18th century, incorporating what remained of various medieval castles. Purchased by Ireland's wealthy and well-known Guinness family in the mid-18th century, it became the minor capital of an estate with 26,000 acres of land. It was sold in 1939 and subsequently converted into one of the island's most famous hotels. In 1952, the stars of one of John Ford's most famous movies (*The Quiet Man*) stayed at this castle. It was sold again and restored in 1970, and the surrounding farms – nearly all of which had been divested – were doubled to create an estate with 350 acres of land and woods. It was sold again in 1985, this time to Irish-American investors who had it decorated lavishly. Ashford can also be reached by boat. The castle has 83 exquisitely decorated rooms with priceless furnishings, intricate wooden carvings, antique furniture, paintings, porcelains, and lovely fireplaces. (G.R.)

82 top and center Ashford is decorated entirely with period furniture. Naturally, the rooms in the most expensive hotel on the Emerald Isle are luxurious and elegant. The images shows two views of the dining room.

82 bottom and 82-83 The Oak Hall is the most important room in the hotel. It is completely paneled in oak and decorated with works by famous painters, Renaissance ceramics and Oriental porcelain, and furniture from the 17th and 18th centuries. A single enormous carpet covers the floor.

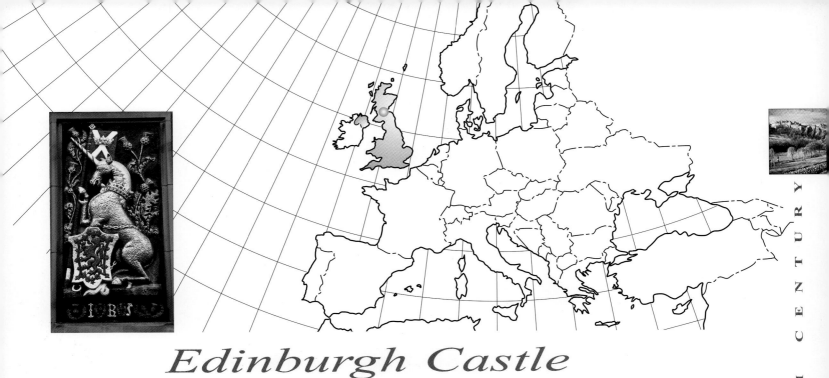

Edinburgh Castle
SCOTLAND

Because of its hillside position facing the sea, the capital of Scotland has been compared to Athens. By the same token, its castle – set on a rocky outcropping with a sheer drop on three sides – bears a striking resemblance to the Acropolis. There is evidence of prehistoric settlements on this rugged and easily defended plateau. Based on monastic chronicles, it was the site of the *Castrum Puellarum* or Castle of the Maidens, used by the Pict rulers as a safe residence for their daughters during wartime. Edwin, the first Christian king of Northumbria, built a fortress here during the 7th century and called it Edwin's Burgh, the origin of the name of the city. The first Scottish ruler to use the fortress as a residence was Malcolm Canmore. His wife Margaret, who died here in 1093, was canonized in 1251. Because of Edinburgh's proximity to the English border, England and Scotland often fought over it, and the castle changed hands several times during the 13th and 14th centuries.

Many key events in Scotland's history took place here. In 1439, seven-year-old King James II was smuggled from the castle, hidden in a trunk by his mother to escape the malevolent Chancellor Crichton. A year later, the boy king attended what went down in history as the Black Dinner, during which the Earl of Douglas, a guest at the castle, was betrayed and murdered. In 1566, Mary Stuart gave birth in the castle to James VI, who would later become King James I of England. Just a few days later, the queen saved her newborn from a plot against his life by lowering him down the side of the castle in a basket. Mary escaped, only to be captured and later imprisoned in England (where she was beheaded in 1587), and in 1573, the castle was desperately defended by her last followers, whose commander was hanged despite the fact that he had surrendered.

In 1650, Cromwell captured the castle after a short siege. In 1745, the garrison refused to open its gates to Prince Charles Edward Stuart, the Young Pretender ("Bonnie Prince Charlie"), who futilely attempted to reclaim the Scottish throne for his heirs. During the Napoleonic Wars, countless French prisoners were locked up in the castle. (G.G.)

84 As dark in color as the rocky cliff on which it was built, Edinburgh Castle is located on a plateau over the city that developed around it.

85 top Scotland has three emblems: the unicorn, the blue flag with the white cross of Saint Andrew, Scotland's patron saint, and the lion rampant within an orle. Stylized thistles are also used to represent Scotland.

85 bottom In this 17th-century bird's-eye view, the castle looks even more impressive, towering over the little houses of Edinburgh.

86-87 The castle's complex walls rise to a height of 500 feet above the gardens on Princess Street. The rooftops of the castle emerge over the top of the walls. It was built in the 15th century and subsequently remodeled.

86 bottom The Great Hall, which boasts an enormous fireplace supported by six columns, houses 16th- and 17th-century weapons and armor, including a bronze cannon.

Edinburgh Castle

Edinburgh Castle was considered one of the most impregnable in Great Britain. Due to continuous remodeling, little remains of the medieval structure. The current buildings look as if they have been compressed between the bastioned walls, which follow the outline of the rocky crest overlooking the city. Despite the fact that it still houses a garrison – a famous military parade is held here every year – the castle is no longer a royal residence. Today it houses a museum that is a popular attraction among visitors, who flock to the Royal Palace and St. Margaret's Chapel. There is a dry moat in front of the main entrance. The most important buildings are set around the *Palace Yard*, including the apartments where Mary Stuart gave birth to James I. The Scottish Crown Jewels are also kept here (they were "lost" for years until Sir Walter Scott discovered them in a secret room), and there are splendid collections of weapons and armor. One of the most famous items at the castle is the massive cannon made in the Netherlands in the 17th century and considered one of the symbols of Scotland: *Mons Meg*. As an insult to the Scottish, it was brought to the Tower of London in 1754. It was returned to the castle – to the joy of Edinburgh's citizens – in 1829. (G.R.)

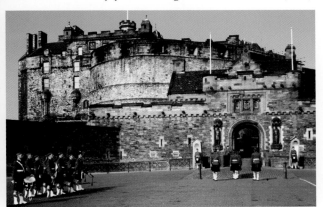

87 top *The entrance, built during the Victorian era and flanked by the statues of two Scottish heroes, William Wallace and Robert the Bruce, opens onto the Esplanade, the large square where military tattoos are held.*

87 bottom *The royal insignias of Scotland are displayed in the Crown Room: the crown, which James V had remade in 1540, the scepter that James IV received from Pope Alexander VI in 1494, and the sword presented to James IV in 1507 by Pope Julius II.*

Glamis Castle
SCOTLAND

William Shakespeare can be credited with making Glamis Castle famous around the world: he used it as the setting for the tragic tale of Macbeth, who supposedly murdered King Duncan here. In reality, the castle did not even exist during the time of Macbeth and his royal victim. It was not until 1372 that King Robert II granted the estate to Sir John Lyon, who then married the king's daughter, Joanna. Sir John had a hunting lodge built here, later enlarging and embellishing it. In the early 16th century, the Lyons fell into disgrace.

When John, the sixth Lord of Glamis, died, his wife was accused of witchcraft, locked in a dark cell so long that she went blind, and finally burnt at the stake in front of Edinburgh castle.

Her young son was also imprisoned, and Glamis was confiscated by the Scottish crown. King James V, Mary Stuart's father, installed his court here from 1537 to 1542. When the king died, the Lord of Glamis was released and his property was returned to him, but all that was left was an empty shell.

The Scottish royal family had taken all its furnishings and silver. John, the eighth Lord of Glamis and Chancellor of Scotland, restored his ancestral castle to its former glory. His descendant Patrick, who became Earl of Strathmore in 1677, had the castle rebuilt as it appears today. The late Queen Mother, the daughter of the fourteenth Earl of Strathmore, lived here for many years, and Princess Margaret, the sister of Queen Elizabeth II, was born here in 1930.

Three ghosts supposedly haunt the castle: the ghost of Lady Glamis, burned at the stake as a witch, the ghost of the Gray Lady, who died of a broken heart, and the ghost of Earl Beardie, a bearded giant who played cards with the devil and lost. (G.G.)

88-89 The rooftop of Glamis Castle - like those of all Scottish baronial castles - boasts a profusion of decorative features: towers, dormers, gables, chimneys, and conical roofs surround the old chemin de ronde like a stone forest.

89 bottom This photograph shows the dizzying spired roofs that end in imaginative, geometric, fancyful sculptures.

90 top The enormous oak-paneled dining room, with large family portraits on the walls, was completed between 1851 and 1853 in the wing of the castle that was rebuilt in the late 1700s.

90 bottom Built between 1773 and 1776, the billiards room is decorated with priceless 17th-century tapestries and fitted bookshelves. The stuccowork on the ceiling is more recent and was done in 1903.

Even in the smallest castles in the loneliest reaches of the Highlands, Scottish architecture always has semi-military features that are medieval in origin and are thus often older than those seen in England. Despite significant French influence, later Scottish castles have unique features, such as the typical L-shaped tower-houses like the one at Glamis. The tower was divided into two or three main stories by barrel vaults and vaulting ribs, and further subdivided into four to six wooden mezzanines. The ancient tower-house of Glamis was rugged and massive in order to protect it against raids by enemy clans. During the 17th century, the third Earl of Strathmore had the interior splendidly decorated and landscaped the grounds, but the castle's fame is linked to countless legends about it. The most famous one involves a mysterious secret room that has never been discovered. During a party in the early 1900s, the Earl of Strathmore decided to look for it and asked his guests to go to every room in the castle and hang a white sheet from each window. When they were done, the group assembled in the garden. They were astonished to discover seven windows that had no white cloth fluttering from them. (G.R.)

*Glamis
Castle*

90-91 A series of portraits hangs on the pink walls of the living room, which has a vaulted ceiling decorated with stuccowork. There is also a large family portrait of the third duke of Strathmore with his children.

91 bottom The daughter of the fourteenth Earl of Strathmore, who married the future King George VI in 1923, became mother of Queen Elizabeth II. The photograph shows the drawing room of her apartments.

Cardiff Castle

WALES

Cardiff Castle's typically Victorian appearance can be attributed to architect William Burges, who fulfilled the wishes of its owner, the third Earl of Bute, for a medieval-looking structure. Nevertheless, the castle is genuinely historic as it dates back to the Romans, who occupied southern Wales and built a *castrum* to keep the recently conquered Celts in check.

The Normans, in turn, built a stone castle, enclosed by a palisade, over the ruins of what had been little more than a redoubt. Robert, the eldest son of William the Conqueror, supposedly died here after being held prisoner for 30 years. In 1158, the indomitable Welsh made a fool out of the Norman castellan. Ifor Bach, the daring and insolent Lord of Senghennyd, launched a surprise attack and captured the castle's unprepared owner and his consort, keeping the couple in chains "until they made amends for the injustices inflicted on the people." Toward the end of the 13th century, Gilbert de Clare rebuilt virtually the entire castle.

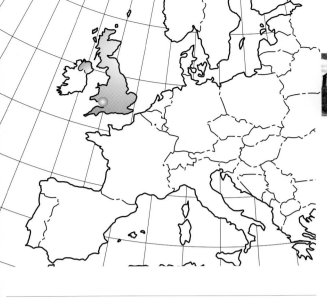

93 top The castle is located at the end of the extensive Bute Park, just outside the city center, and is surrounded by thick walls with a rectangular layout.

93 bottom The Welsh insignia, a red dragon on a white-green field, flutters from the Norman keep in the middle of the complex.

When the Welsh-born Henry VII (1485-1507), founder of England's Tudor dynasty took over the castle in 1490, the interior was renovated to turn it into a noble residence. In 1551, Edward VI donated it to Sir William Herbert, one of the ancestors of the Earls of Bute, who owned it from 1790 to 1947, when it was turned over to the city government. (G.G.)

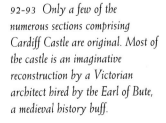

92-93 Only a few of the numerous sections comprising Cardiff Castle are original. Most of the castle is an imaginative reconstruction by a Victorian architect hired by the Earl of Bute, a medieval history buff.

92 bottom Coats of arms and polychrome statues decorate the murder holes and lancet windows of the Clock Tower, which now houses a music and drama school.

94-95 Twenty-two frescoed paintings and stained-glass windows, portraying the different lords of Cardiff over the centuries, decorate the Banqueting Hall, which has an enormous castle-shaped fireplace on the main wall.

94 bottom The lively decorations that delighted the Earl of Bute are evident everywhere: this phantasmagoria of medieval scenes, with gleaming gold and enamel work, is in the Winter Smoking Room.

Cardiff Castle

The "most singular construction of the Victorian period," located in the heart of Cardiff, was built for John Patrick Crichton-Stuart, the third Earl of Bute, who transformed the city into the country's most important coal-exporting port. This trade made the Earl immensely wealthy and, in fact, he was considered the richest man of his era. Fascinated with the Middle Ages, he wanted a residence that would embody all the legendary aspects of those faraway times. Despite the fact that several sections of its walls are 2,000 years old, the castle was one of the first examples of Gothic revival. Architect William Burges added five towers to the 18th-century body of the castle, including the spectacular *Clock Tower*. Every room was decorated with a breathtaking profusion of ornamentation inspired by different themes. In addition to Arabic and Indian décors, the castle even had Mediterranean gardens. In the *Herbert Tower's Arab Room*, for example, the ceilings were ornately decorated and the marble fireplaces were studded with semiprecious stones such as lapis lazuli and pink quartz. The leading craftsmen of the day were hired to create the banquet halls, and special care was lavished on the library and its collection of extremely rare books. (G.R.)

95 top *The library is the simplest room in the castle. It is arranged like a typical monastic library, with "Gothic" shelves holding priceless books.*

95 bottom *The medieval motif was even used in the children's rooms. The nursery of the scions of the Earl of Bute is decorated with a long procession of figures, inspired by Romanesque paintings, around the upper part of the walls.*

Windsor Castle

ENGLAND

96 top King Edward III, depicted here in 19th-century copy of an anonymous portrait now at Hampton Court, had the castle torn down in the 12th century to build a completely new one.

96 bottom Windsor is the largest and most important castle in England, the name later adopted by the royal family. The castle, just a few miles outside London, is set on a limestone hill overlooking the right bank of the Thames.

The House of Hanover, which had ruled Great Britain since 1714, adopted the surname Windsor in 1914 to quell anti-German sentiments during the deadly war against Germany. The name came from the town of Windsor, which was an insignificant Saxon village in 1070, the year William the Conqueror bought it from the monks of Westminster Abbey. He built a wooden fortress controlling one of the bends of the River Thames in order to protect London from any enemies arriving from the west. Henry I (1100-35) and Henry II (1154-89) rebuilt it in stone and significantly expanded the stronghold, adding several towers. However, Edward III (1327-77), who was born in Windsor, had the previous buildings demolished and ordered the ones still standing today. Architect William of Wykeham was commissioned for this work, which he directed for 19 years – from 1356 to 1374 – for the salary of one shilling a day. The

96-97 Windsor Castle closely resembles the original 14th-century structure, and its current appearance is the result of the general restoration work done by George III and George IV in the early 1800s.

97 bottom Windsor - portrayed here in a 17th-century engraving by Georg Hoefnagel from the work Civitates Orbis Terrarum - is more of a small, independent urban complex than a palace. It has always been a royal residence and center of power.

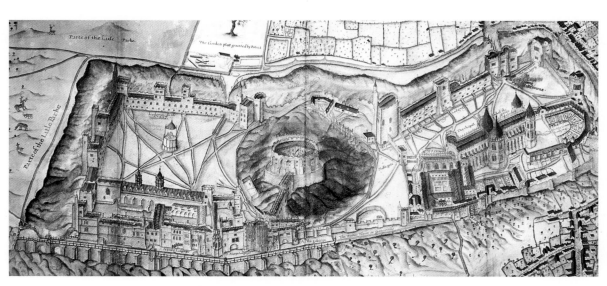

workmen received food but no wages. They were poor people taken from the streets of the kingdom by the king's footmen and forced to work. Anyone who tried to escape to return home was arrested and jailed as a traitor and felon. Edward III also built quarters there for the Military Knights of Windsor, the chivalric order he founded alongside the Royal Order of the Garter, which met in St. George's Chapel, dedicated to the order's patron saint. The rebuilding of the chapel began a century later, in 1474, under Edward IV (1461-83) and was continued by Henry VIII (1509-47). Edward IV also founded St. George's College and the Horseshoe Cloisters, a semicircular building that housed the chapel canons. Henry VIII had the main entrance built. The royal apartments were completely restructured under Charles II (1660-85) between 1675 and 1683, giving them a more lavish appearance. However, Windsor was neglected by the king's successors until George III (1760-1820) fully renovated the castle at the turn of the 19th century. He commissioned architect James Wyatt, whose nephew, Jeffry Wyattville, continued the work under George IV (1820-30) and greatly accentuated its neo-Gothic aspects. The artwork in the castle was nearly destroyed in 1992 when a fire broke out in Queen Elizabeth II's private chapel and spread to the royal apartments. It took 24 hours to put out the flames. (G.G.)

98 top and bottom Proud of its traditions, Great Britain cherishes the magnificent royal ceremonies that have fallen into disuse elsewhere or have been greatly scaled back. Windsor Castle is often used for state visits, parades, and celebrations, which are held in the large area between the buildings and attract crowds of onlookers from London.

Windsor Castle

98-99 The age-old trees in the majestic English park create a marvelous backdrop for the long palisade, with battlemented towers rising above it. The round shape of the Norman keep is visible on the left. A staircase with 220 steps leads to the top of the tower.

99 bottom St. George's Chapel, dedicated to the patron saint of the Royal Order of the Garter, is an English-Gothic masterpiece. Construction began in 1478 under Henry Jenyns and was completed by William Vertue in 1511.

Everything is grand in this royal palace, which is unanimously considered the most important example of a residence that has been occupied uninterruptedly since the Middle Ages. Its layout is still based on two baileys set next to the original Norman motte built on a chalky hill overlooking the Thames. The original structures were subsequently connected by buildings added by virtually every English king. The entire complex, enclosed by a long wall dotted with a variety of different towers, is surrounded by a huge park. One of the most notable sections is the enormous keep restored by Sir Jeffry Wyattville (architect of George IV), who spent one million pounds to build the tallest tower in the kingdom. The rooms are exquisitely decorated with masterpieces from the royal collection (the largest private collection in the world, with priceless works such as drawings by Leonardo da Vinci and portraits by Hans Holbein). One of the most important rooms is the *Waterloo Chamber*, designed by Wyattville to display the portraits of the monarchs, statesmen and generals who helped defeat Napoleon. The floor of this room is covered by an extraordinary carpet that was woven at Agra and is one of the largest in the world. The impressive St. George's Chapel was built in honor of the Royal Order of the Garter. (G.R.)

Windsor Castle

100-101 *The interior of St. George's Chapel, which is as tall as it is wide, is divided into a nave and two aisles by rows of pillars that rise to the vault and then fan out to form complicated star-shaped figures.*

101 top *St. George's Hall which is, over 180 feet long, is the ceremonial hall of the Royal Order of the Garter. The knights' armor lines its walls, which are decorated with portraits of the monarchs.*

101 bottom left *The choir in St. George's Chapel, enclosed by 19th-century Gothic-style wooden railings, holds the stalls and heraldic insignias of the knights of the Royal Order of the Garter. The Order first started meeting here in 1348.*

101 bottom right *In the Throne Room, a gilded carved chair with the letters "E.R." ("Elizabeth Regina" in Latin, in keeping with tradition) awaits Her Majesty under a velvet canopy.*

102 top The State Apartments are used to host official ceremonies and are richly decorated with antique furniture and artwork. This is a corner of the Crimson Drawing Room.

102 bottom The Queen's Ballroom, one of the most lavishly decorated rooms in the castle, has beautiful paintings, including landscapes by Canaletto, and portraits by Hogarth, Ramsey, and Gainsborough.

102-103 An enormous carpet, woven especially in Agra, India, for this room covers the floor of the Green Drawing Room, which is decorated with Georgian furniture and mirrors reflecting the dazzling chandeliers.

103 bottom left The Waterloo Chamber features portraits of the figures who helped topple Napoleon, England's relentless enemy. Most of the works are by Lawrence.

103 bottom right The countless rooms in the immense living complex are exquisitely decorated, and each one can be considered a miniature museum.

Windsor Castle

Warwick Castle

ENGLAND

104 As legend would have it, Warwick Castle was founded in 915 by Princess Ethelfleda, daughter of Alfred the Great. However, it is more likely that it was built by William the Conqueror.

104-105 Warwick Castle, overlooking the Avon, watched over traffic along the river. Though it was remodeled several times, most of the castle looks like it did in the 14th century. Its enormous walls are 10 to 20 feet thick.

Located in the Midlands – the very heart of England – just a few miles from Shakespeare's birthplace, Stratford-upon-Avon, Warwick is one of the kingdom's most picturesque feudal castles. According to tradition, it was founded in 915 by Princess Ethelfleda, daughter of Alfred the Great (871-899), the king of Wessex, which then dominated the other Anglo-Saxon states. However, William the Conqueror (1066-87), the Norman who invaded England in 1066, may actually have founded it in 1068 to help maintain control over the region. William entrusted the stronghold to Baron Henry, Lord of Newbourg in Normandy, who was named Earl of Warwick.

A 15th-century genealogist subsequently "traced" the family's illustrious ancestors, including Brutus and Guy of Warwick, the legendary Anglo-Saxon warrior.

105 bottom Located in the Midlands, the city of Warwick - like its castle - has maintained the appearance of bygone days, with lovely old houses surrounded by greenery and dominated by the castle towers.

Many great figures have borne the title of Earl of Warwick, and some of them have played key roles in English history. One of the most important was Richard Neville (1428-1471), referred to as "the Kingmaker" because of his role in the War of the Roses between the houses of Lancaster and York, which were vying for the throne. His predecessor Richard Beauchamp was also a notable figure. A young knight-errant who traveled to the Holy Land, he crossed Eastern Europe – which was largely barbarian at the time – and competed in tournaments (his victory over Pandolfo Malatesta in Verona is legendary). He also participated in the Hundred Years War against France, and in 1430 he oversaw the trial of Joan of Arc in Rouen. His tomb at Warwick, in St. Mary's Church, is a masterpiece of 15th-century English sculpture. (G.G.)

Inhabited since the 14th century, Warwick Castle still looks like a medieval fortress. However, its interior was transformed during the 17th and 18th centuries, and it was renovated so lavishly and elegantly that it is now considered a true residential palace. The castle walls, which are magnificently preserved, are 10 to 20 feet thick and still feature all their 14th-century defensive structures. A rare turret referred to as a "crow's nest," which was used as a guard tower, still stands next to *Clarence Tower*. The entrance – the weak point of any castle – and the barbican were ingeniously fortified. Warwick Castle's towers are considered among the most dramatic in England. The oldest is *Guy's Tower*, which was built in the 14th century and is 131 feet tall. Canaletto painted five views of the castle between 1748 and 1752, when it was renovated and a garden was added. The Great Hall, chapel, dining room, library, and music room are especially interesting, with valuable collections of furniture, tapestries, carpets, paintings and statues. Warwick is one of the most popular of England's many castles and hosts a variety of special events and historical commemorations. (G.R.)

106 top The fantastic animals of dazzling medieval heraldry stand out on the stained-glass windows of one of the rooms in the castle.

106 bottom An enormous Venetian table, with carved legs portraying pregnant women, stands in the middle of the Cedar Room, paneled with Lebanese cedar and decorated with portraits by Van Dyck and Lely.

106-107 The Great Hall, which is over 360 feet long, certainly lives up to its name. Overlooking the Avon, it offers visitors a breathtaking view, as well as a rich collection of 16th- and 17th-century weapons and armor.

Warwick Castle

107 bottom The equestrian portrait of King Charles I, by Van Dyck (left), is the highlight of the State Dining Room, where banquets were held. The Two Lions by Rubens, hanging over the fireplace, is also striking.

108 *Bamburgh Castle is one of the oldest in England. It dates back to the 6th century, when the Saxons* *conquered Northumbria and established the capital of one of their kingdoms here.*

Bamburgh Castle
ENGLAND

In 410, when Rome abandoned its province of Britannia, no longer being able to maintain legions to defend it, increasing numbers of Jutes, Angles, and Saxons started to land on its coasts. The Celts, led by Arthur (of whom the popular historical record is dubious), were driven into Wales and the newcomers established seven kingdoms. One of them, Northumbria, was conquered in 547 by King Ida the Flamebearer, who established his capital at Bamburgh and built a small fortress surrounded by a palisade. This rough fortification was not transformed into a true castle until after 1066, when William the Conqueror (1066-87) and his Normans had overrun Anglo-Saxon England and built numerous strongholds in strategic positions to ensure their control of the country.

A few years later, Bamburgh was the site of the battle between the Conqueror's son, William Rufus (1087-1100) and Robert of Normandy for the English crown. William laid siege to Robert's castle and built another fortress across from it, ironically calling it Malveisin, or "Evil Neighbor," and Bamburgh finally surrendered. The castle and its territory were part of the royal demesne until the time of Elizabeth I, who granted the property to Claudius Forster to reward him for his services in these frontier areas, which were full of cattle thieves and villains who took advantage of the border nearby to flee into Scotland and escape punishment. Claudius Forster was so delighted with this gift that he lived at Bamburgh for the rest of his life, dying there at the age of 101, and leaving behind eleven sons and two daughters.

One of Claudius' descendants, Tom Forster, participated in the Jacobite rebellion in 1715, which sought to win back the throne for Britain's ousted Stuart dynasty. However, when he led his men to the battlefield to face the enemy, he realized that he was greatly outnumbered and promptly surrendered without firing a single shot. Back at the castle, his sister Dorothy was informed that her brother had been taken prisoner and she began to visit him every day, accompanied by one of her maidservants. His jailers became so accustomed to seeing these two daily visitors that Tom managed to escape, disguised in the maid's clothes. The fugitive went to France, but his family was ruined and was forced to sell the castle. It was purchased by Lord Crewe, Bishop of Durham, who set up a school to train girls for domestic service. Toward the end of the 19th century, the complex was sold to Lord Armstrong, who restored it extensively to its current appearance. (G.G.)

Perched on a volcanic outcropping facing the stormy North Sea, Bamburgh is probably the most striking and dramatic castle in England. Its breathtaking appearance is accentuated by the color of the old medieval stronghold, which was built in red sandstone. Over the years, the castle gradually expanded to cover an area of five acres. The massive square keep in the middle is surrounded by walls, with towers, bartizans (small projecting turrets), curtain walls, and ramparts. However, little remains of the famous fortress of the War of the Roses, because Lord Armstrong remodeled it into a baronial residence during the Victorian period. Nevertheless, the interior reflects the Tudor style, resembling the structures at Longridge and Tilmouth Park. The distinctive Norman arches of the keep, as well as the vaults in the Great Hall, are still visible. Bamburgh is now the residence of the Armstrong family, but many of its stately and ornately decorated rooms are open to visitors. There are also two museums there. The first one, which is quite unusual, displays various items and artifacts connected with the first Baron Armstrong and his work as an engineer, while the second one features memorabilia about the history of aviation. (G.R.)

108-109 The castle was reconstructed by Lord Armstrong during the Victorian era, in order to restore its old Norman appearance.

109 bottom The castle walls surround the keep, which is defended by four towers. Bamburgh, dominating the North Sea shore, paints a striking picture.

110 Dover Castle, which
dominates the city from a
hilltop, was hurriedly built by
the Saxon king Harold to ward
off the imminent Norman
invasion, but it was not enough
to stop the attack.

Dover Castle

ENGLAND

The castle stands out on the "white cliffs of Dover" celebrated by all those who enter England via this historic port. England's last Anglo-Saxon ruler, King Harold, built the castle in 1064 to defend what was considered the island's main gateway, but neither the castle nor the adjoining coastal region was sufficiently fortified to stop William the Conqueror, who with his Normans invaded England in 1066. The Normans transformed the original settlement into a powerful complex, making the port increasingly important from a trade and military standpoint. Between 1168 and 1174, King Henry II (1154-89) further reinforced the castle by building the keep and the internal curtain wall, and Henry III (1216-72) added the exterior walls. As a result, in 1216 King John successfully withstood the long, tenacious siege by the joint forces of the French Dauphin and the rebellious barons. During the Civil Wars that raged across England from 1642 to 1649, culminating with the beheading of Charles I and the proclamation of the republic, the Parliamentarians tricked the Royalists into surrendering the castle. In a strange twist of fate, however, this is precisely where Charles II landed in 1660 with the re-establishment of the monarchy following Cromwell's death. The castle was remodeled and enlarged in the 1800-1810 period to avert the threatened Napoleonic invasion, which never took place.

Because of its location, Dover has also played an important role in the history of aviation. In 1785, John Jeffries and Jean-Pierre Blanchard took off from the clearing in front of the castle walls in a hot-air balloon. The first people to fly across the English Channel, they landed in the woods near Calais after a 150-minute flight. Frenchman Louis Blériot completed the first plane crossing from Calais to Dover on July 25, 1909: his flight took just 38 minutes. (G.G.)

squat construction an oddly graceful vertical appearance. The interior is divided by a cruciform hall. There are four main rooms, each one 50 by 20 feet, and 12 rooms that are 13 to 16 by 10 feet and were hollowed out from the castle walls. There are two chapels, set one over the other, in the southeast corner. The entrance is a characteristic round arch decorated with jagged zigzag motifs, or chevrons, typical of Norman architecture. Curiously, the exterior defenses of this stone "bestiary" also evoke a jaw-like image. In fact, the concrete "dragon's teeth" set up in 1940 in fear of the Nazi invasion are still visible. They act as a reminder to what has often been the sad fate of castles: continuous reuse. (G.R.)

Dover Castle is protected on three sides by a deep ditch and two curtain walls. The fourth side is defended by an impassable obstacle: the sea. Henry III added the Constable's Gate in 1216. The central keep – rugged and massive – is distinctive of Norman architecture (its entrance resembles the one at Rochester Castle on the Thames estuary). It is a stone cube with four corner towers and four foreparts projecting between the towers, thus giving the

111 top The keep, built between 1180 and 1186, is one of the most impressive in English architecture. The elegant upper chapel, built in the late-Norman style, is delicately outlined by arches and ribbing.

111 bottom King Henry III added the outer walls between 1230 and 1240, in order to reinforce the defensive structures of what had become the main gateway to the kingdom of England.

122 *The stables, covered by broad Gothic arches supported by columns, look exactly the way they did in the 12th century, when they were built by Count Philip.*

Gravensteen
BELGIUM

The Count of Flanders, Arnulf I (918-965), chose a tall sandy dune surrounded by the waters of the River Lys as the place to build a wooden fortress. It was protected by a palisade and equipped with warehouses to store grain and other foodstuffs to sustain the populace in the event of an attack. The city of Ghent developed around this little stronghold and the two nearby abbeys founded by Saint Amand three centuries earlier to evangelize the region. The counts rebuilt their stronghold in stone in about the year 1000. Starting in the early 13th century, Ghent became famous across Europe for its cloth. This industry enriched artisans and the middle classes, and it also filled the counts' coffers.

Following a terrible fire, Count Philip reconstructed the castle in 1180, making extensive changes and elevating the central keep – the donjon – to a height of nearly 100 feet, so that it towered over Ghent's rich noble residences aligned on the opposite bank of the Lys. During the 14th century, the merchant classes helped make Ghent the most important city in Flanders by forging a close alliance with the kings of England. In fact, wool from English flocks provided the raw material for weaving cloth, and England then purchased the finished products.

Throughout the 14th century, the counts clashed openly with their subjects over political power, as Ghent's trade guilds had become so prosperous they demanded a democratic government. The city and the castle overlooking it became enemies, and Count Louis de Male (1346-1384) finally decided to move his residence elsewhere. However, the castle remained the administrative center of Flanders, housing the superior court, which was installed in 1407. The county's most important ceremonies were held here not only during this

period but also under the rule of the Dukes of Burgundy. The establishment of the Order of the Golden Fleece, created to defend the legendary and poetic deeds of chivalry, was also celebrated here. It was not until the 18th century, during the Austrian period, that the governor of the Netherlands lost interest in the castle and decided to sell it. It was purchased by an industrialist, who set up a metalworking factory and a spinning mill in it, and some of the buildings were used to house workers. At the end of the 19th century, after risking demolition as the "symbol of feudal oppression," the castle was purchased by the city of Ghent. Joseph De Waele restored it and tried to recreate its 12th-century appearance, but most of the details that give it such a "medieval" air are purely products of the architect's imagination. (G.G.)

Gravensteen in its current form can be attributed to Philip of Alsace, Count of Flanders from 1157 to 1191. He had the unusual cruciform opening made over the main entrance to commemorate his departure for the Crusades, from which he never returned.

An enormous and impressive elliptical curtain wall with 24 cylindrical towers encloses approximately one acre of land. There are two fortified structures inside it: the donjon and the count's quarters. The donjon is the oldest of its kind in Europe, and it boasts extraordinary Romanesque windows with round arches supported by slender columns.

In the past, temporary wooden structures could be added inside the keep and the outside towers for two-level defense. Even today, the complex is surrounded by a wide moat. (G.R.)

122-123 *The castle resembles an enormous stone complex enclosed by crenellated curtain walls. The keep, with projecting corner towers, and the sturdy ravelin rise majestically above the walls.*

123 bottom *The wall, set between two small towers with conical roofs, has two rows of Romanesque windows with round arches, supported by slender columns.*

114-115 *During the 17th century, a bastioned fortress was built around the medieval castle to defend Holland against the French forces. The bastions have now been transformed into gardens.*

115 top *Following extensive and patient restoration work, Muiderslot now looks like it did at the end of the 14th century, when Albert, the Count of Holland, rebuilt it over the foundations of a previous castle.*

Muiderslot
NETHERLANDS

The first castle at Muiden was built by Floris V, Count of Holland, in about 1280. His objective was to control the estuary of the Vecht River, which flowed into what was then the Zuiderzee, the great inland sea that has now been partially reclaimed. Floris decided that he would charge a toll on boats passing through on their way from Utrecht, whose bishops were the count's enemies. A few years later – in 1296 – Floris was captured by a group of rebellious nobles and imprisoned in his own castle. His captors, threatened when the castle was besieged, fled with the count and killed him. The bishop of Utrecht took advantage of his rival's death to raze his fortress. However, its position was too strategic to be left unguarded, and in 1370 Albert, the Count of Holland, had the current complex built over the foundations of the original one. Perhaps mindful of his predecessor's misfortune, Albert never lived there and had a knight commander and a small garrison installed at Muiderslot.

The castle's most famous knight commander was the poet and historian Pieter Cornelisz Hooft (1581-1647), who lived there from 1609 until 1647 and hosted some of the most famous figures of 17th-century Holland, including Hugo de Groot, Constantijn Huygens, and Joost van den Vondel, the country's most important poet. This group of writers, philosophers, and scientists was referred to as the Muiden Circle. The castle's current furnishings date back to this period. Toward the end of 17th century, major work was done to modernize Muiderslot, since it held the key position in a fortified line to defend Holland from the expansionist aims of Louis XIV. In fact, the Dutch blocked an invading French army at Muiderslot by artificially flooding the territory they had to cross. A century later, the castle was in such poor condition that the decision was made to demolish it and reuse its masonry and other materials, but King Willem I banned its destruction. However, restoration work did not begin until 1895. Further restoration work was conducted between 1948 and 1972, and Muiderslot has now been converted into a museum and center for cultural events. (G.G.)

Muiderslot is probably the most famous castle in Holland. A rugged fortified site existed here as early as the 11th century.

Its appearance today is the result of repeated restoration work. Built entirely of bricks, the castle has a square ground plan with circular towers at the the four corners and a square tower set in the middle of the façade and is surrounded by a wide moat. Numerous landscape painters from the 17th to the 20th centuries considered it to be among their favorite subjects.

Muiderslot is a rather small castle – just 105 by 115 feet – with walls that are five feet thick. Its beautiful rooms were restored to recreate their original 17th-century appearance, and they house a valuable collection of weapons and armor. It now houses a national museum and folklore events, conventions, and ceremonies are held here. (G.R.)

Muiderslot

116-117 The castle's enormous halls, with coffered ceilings, now house a national museum with paintings and furnishings, mainly from the 16th and 17th centuries.

117 top A bookstand with an open prayer book, an elegant canopy bed and a painted cradle at the foot of the bed: this is the bedroom of a pious chatelaine.

117 bottom The lords of the castle and their courtiers would meet in the Rittersaal, or Knights' Hall, and sit in front of the fireplace decorated with typical Dutch tiles.

Neuschwanstein

GERMANY

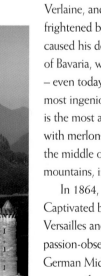

The "king of fairy tales" according to his adoring subjects, "the only true king of this century" according to poet Paul Verlaine, and the "mad king" according to his ministers who, frightened by his outlandish spending, finally deposed him and caused his death. We're talking about morbid, eccentric Ludwig II of Bavaria, who is widely admired – and equally widely criticized – even today. Anyone who visits the castle of Neuschwanstein, his most ingenious creation, is bound to think that the first definition is the most appropriate. Indeed, this faux medieval castle covered with merlons and spires, which materializes like an apparition in the middle of an evergreen forest backed by snowcapped mountains, inspired Walt Disney's cartoon fairy tales.

In 1864, at the age of 19, Ludwig became king of Bavaria. Captivated by the historic legend of the Sun King, the pomp of Versailles and the music of Wagner, he shared the composer's passion-obsession for an idealized rather than factual image of the German Middle Ages. The same legends that inspired Wagner's operas – the saga of Parsifal and the Holy Grail, the Nibelungen and the Swan Knight Lohengrin – are the subjects of the decorative cycles in the halls of Neuschwanstein, the first of three castles built by Ludwig and the last one to be completed. Construction, directed by architects Riedel and Dollmann based on plans drawn up by set designer Jank, began in 1869 and was completed in 1886, but only because the king died that year. The rooms on the top floors were thus left empty and bare. In June of that year, Ludwig's ministers accused him of squandering the country's money on his increasingly mad and extravagant architectural dreams. The ministers' claims were certainly grounded, and they deposed him by having a leading Bavarian physician declare Ludwig mentally ill, despite the fact that the doctor had never even seen the king.

118 top Handsome, erudite, and sophisticated, Ludwig II of Bavaria, shown here in a youthful portrait, paid more attention to his passion for architecture than to running the country. This ultimately cost him his throne - and his life.

118 bottom The castle of Neuschwanstein, with its red brick entrance and pure white walls, rises like a fairy-tale apparition, ringed by the green Bavarian Alps.

118-119 Snow and winter fog accentuate the surreal aura surrounding the castle, which was the most expensive and outrageously sumptuous of the three built by Ludwig.

119 bottom The work required an enormous amount of materials, complicated excavations, and roadwork in order to transport the materials to the steep location chosen for the castle. This photograph from 1875 shows the construction work.

Ludwig was respectfully but firmly taken from Neuschwanstein and moved to Berg Castle on Lake Starnberg, where he was closely guarded. Though the water was no more than five feet deep, Ludwig's body was found in the lake on July 13: he and his doctor had drowned. According to some theories, he committed suicide, whereas according to others he had drowned as he tried to escape or was murdered. His cousin, Empress Elizabeth of Austria (Sissi, another legendary figure in the royal tragedies of the 19th century), perhaps the only woman that Ludwig, a homosexual, had ever loved, offered what may well be the only real explanation. "The king wasn't mad. He was simply an eccentric who lived in his own dream world. They should have treated him more kindly." (G.G.)

120 top Behind the altar in the chapel, built in pure neo-Gothic style, there is a painting of St. Louis, the king of France and Ludwig's patron saint. Angels welcome Louis as he ascends to heaven, holding the banner of the crusade during which he was killed.

120 bottom An enormous mosaic reminiscent of the ones in the Palatine Chapel in Palermo decorates the apse in the Throne Room. Below the figure of Christ, six canonized kings represent the divine power bestowed on monarchs. The throne was supposed to be set at the top of a staircase, but it was never installed.

120-121 Divided into two levels, the majestic Throne Room gleams with gold, enamel work, and mosaics, the idealized reconstruction of a Byzantine palace inspired by the Allerheiligenhofkirche (All Saints Church) in Munich.

121 bottom In the middle of the floor of the Throne Room, an impressive, delicate mosaic with stylized animals and plants evokes the miniatures of medieval bestiaries.

122-123 The Singers' Hall features a coffered ceiling painted with ornamental motifs and zodiac signs. It has eight gilded brass chandeliers that, together with the candelabras, hold over 600 candles.

122 bottom One of the spiral staircases inside ends with a sculpture of a dragon, set next to a column with a polychrome capital; the vault depicting a starry sky.

The Allgau area of Bavaria held great strategic importance during the Middle Ages, as demonstrated by the fact that there were once four castles here. This is where Ludwig decided to build his "sublime whipped-cream folly." Preliminary drawings by Count von Pocci and Christian Jank show that the central body of the castle was modeled after the Wartburg. Ludwig II insisted that the building should blend in with its surroundings. From spring to fall, astonishing quantities of materials were transported to the site: over 5,000 tons of Nuerting sandstone, more than 510 tons of Salzburg marble, and 400,000 bricks were used in 1879-80 alone. The entire façade was clad in Alterschrofen limestone. The

Neuschwanstein

furnishings and interior finishing were done by architects who were expert theater designers, stonecutters, painters, and ceramicists, and the total cost exceeded six million marks. The rooms are diverse and overblown. Most of them are decorated with paintings evoking the German sagas and the sacredness of German kings. One example is the *Throne Room*, a Gothic, Romanesque, and Byzantine mélange of mosaics; its crown-shaped brass chandelier weighs over a ton. Apart from the cabinetry masterpieces done in the neo-Gothic style that was so popular during this period, the king insisted on all the latest technical features and gadgets, like electric bells and an ultra-functional kitchen. (G.R.)

123 top The hall is dedicated to the saga of the Swan Knight Lohengrin, whose deeds fascinated the young Ludwig, inspiring him to build the castle of Neuschwanstein.

123 bottom The paintings in the studio, paneled in oak and decorated with oak furniture, illustrate the saga of Tannhäuser. The ceiling is made of inlaid wood.

124 top left The minstrel
Tannhäuser entertains the court of
Hermann of Thuringia at
Wartburg Castle in this fresco by
J. Aigner, painted on one of the
walls of the studio.

124 top right The knight Siegfried is another leading figure of Ludwig's favorite Wagnerian operas, set in the Middle Ages. The knight is depicted battling the Dragon in the fresco by Wilhelm Hauschild, located in the Waiting Room of the Singers' Hall.

124-125 A graceful lady in medieval dress sits under a Gothic arch in the king's bedchamber, reading the tale of Tristan and Isolde. Unlike the rest of the rooms, which are neo-Romanesque, the chamber is decorated in a late Gothic style.

125 The decorations in the Singers' Hall are devoted to the legend of Parsifal, depicted in this 1885 fresco by Ferdinand Piloty the Younger.

Neuschwanstein

126-127 The enormous
Kaiserstallung, the ancient
granary built between 1494 and
1495 and now transformed into a
youth hostel, stands in the middle
of the complex. On the right is the
Fünfeckiger Turm, which in turn
faces the round Sinwellturm.

126 bottom The Burg has
changed very little since 1671, the
year Johann Georg Erasmus
executed this bird's-eye view now
at the Nuremberg City Library.

Kaiserburg

GERMANY

Founded shortly after the year 1000, Nuremberg became a free city of the Holy Roman Empire in 1219 by decree of Frederick II. It was Germany's leading trade city until the 16th century, and goods from the Orient came through here from Venice. Its houses were dominated by two fortresses built on a rocky formation, rival castles that faced each other: Burggrafenburg, owned by the powerful Zoller family, and Kaiserburg, the imperial fortress entrusted to the city. For 300 years, the garrisons of the two castles scowled at each other, and several times they took each other on in armed combat. Unable to subdue the middle classes, which were growing increasingly wealthy and proud of their freedom, in 1427 the Zollers decided to sell Burggrafenburg to the city council. The enemy castles were merged into one, which kept the name of Kaiserburg. The latter had already been declared the imperial residence of Frederick Barbarossa, and until 1571, all the German rulers of the Holy Roman Empire stayed there for a certain period of time. However, the castle was never furnished. Each time the emperor announced his upcoming arrival, the most well-to-do families in this city of merchants were required to lend furnishings, crockery, tapestries, and anything the sovereign and his large retinue might need, and these items were not returned to their owners until the illustrious guests left.

The fortress was never modernized and thus became militarily antiquated. As a result, it was unable to defend the city from the horrors of the Thirty Years War (1618-48). Nevertheless, Nuremberg's decline had started a century earlier, following an era of great splendor. During this period, its fairs attracted buyers from all over Germany, who came here for the city's products, including the famous "Nuremberg eggs," the first pocket watches. During the early 16th century, the Portuguese discovery of the route to the Indies, circling around the Cape of Good Hope, diverted the spice trade from Venice to Lisbon and thus to Antwerp, which replaced Nuremberg as the trading center of Northern Europe. Kaiserburg no longer attracted the magnificent and merry guests from the imperial court, and it was abandoned until restoration work was undertaken in the 19th century. (G.G.)

127 top The imperial fortress essentially looks the same as it did in the 16th century, when the rulers of the Holy Roman Empire often came to stay for extended periods of time.

127 bottom In the intricate urban fabric of Nuremberg, the complex of the fortress stands out with its towers and walls, surrounded by 17th-century bastions now used as a park.

Kaiserburg

Kaiserburg is the main part of the castle. There are two unique architectural details at the far ends of the castle: the Sinwell Tower, which dominates the complex and is the very symbol of the castle, and the massive underground granaries, which were so big they could hold enough wheat to feed the population for centuries. The interior of the castle has fascinating Gothic halls, such as the *Kaisersaal* and the *Rittersaal*, with antique furnishings. The *Doppelkapelle*, or double chapel, is fascinating. It is composed of two connected, consecrated rooms; the upper one used by the emperor and his family whereas the lower one was for commoners. The castle now houses a famous museum displaying a large collection of medieval relics connected with the long dynastic history of the city of Nuremberg (the *Holy Lance*, used by Longino to pierce the chest of Jesus, is kept here). The powerful exterior ramparts were separated by a wide deep moat, and they were designed to eliminate dead corners and permit crossfire. (G.R.)

128 The two-story Romanesque chapel, with a nave and two aisles, was built in the 11th century. From an architectural standpoint, it is the most exquisite part of Kaiserburg castle. The emperors would come here to pray.

129 top The ceiling of the Imperial Reception Hall, restored to its original splendor in 1948 following serious damage caused by bombing during World War II, is decorated with the coats of arms of the emperors and two-headed eagles.

129 bottom left When the rulers were in Nuremberg, parties and banquets would be held in the Kaisersaal, which has completely been reconstructed. Portraits of the emperors and members of the Hapsburg dynasty line the walls.

129 bottom right Lovely 16th-century furniture decorates the salon. The palace was never furnished on a permanent basis. The city's notables were required to provide furniture whenever an emperor announced that he planned to visit.

Marksburg

GERMANY

130-131 *The massive central tower, built in about 1100, is surrounded by buildings that were added later, mainly during the 15th century.*

131 top *The various parts of the castle are arranged stepwise down the slope of the hill towards the rebuilt masonry bridge, which was once a drawbridge.*

131 center *Purchased by the German Castles Association, Marksburg underwent radical restoration. This picture shows one of the wood-paneled bedrooms.*

131 bottom *The Gothic kitchen has long tables set under massive round chandeliers hanging from the beamed ceiling.*

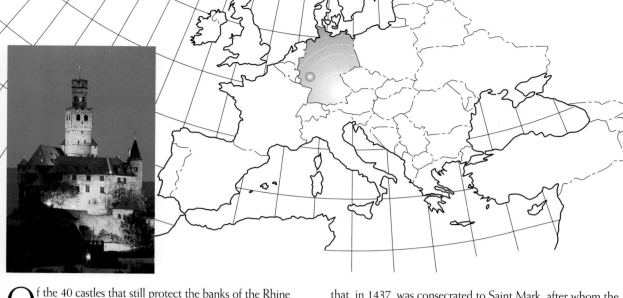

Of the 40 castles that still protect the banks of the Rhine between Bingen and Koblenz, Marksburg is the only one that has never been destroyed. All the rest, often reduced to just their exterior walls by raging enemies or, more simply, by the passage of time, have undergone extensive restoration or were completely reconstructed during the Romantic period. Instead, Marksburg remains a genuine example of a medieval Rhenish fortress. The Eppsteins, one of the region's most powerful families (several of them became the archbishops of Mainz and Trier), built the keep, the original nucleus of the castle, in about 1100. In 1283, Marksburg was purchased by another important figure in medieval Rhineland, Count Eberhard II of Katzenelnbogen, who ordered the work that gave the castle the Gothic appearance we see today.

New additions and transformations were made after 1429 when, following the death of the last of the Katzenelnbogen heirs, the castle was taken over by the counts of Hesse.

The counts wanted to adapt the stronghold to the innovations that had been made in the art of warfare, as the introduction of the cannon made it a decisive weapon of attack for knocking down walls and towers. Later Marksburg lost all importance from a military standpoint, and when Napoleon abolished the Holy Roman Empire in 1803 with the stroke of pen, he gave the castle to his allies, the Dukes of Nassau. In fact its new owners did not use it as a fortress, employing part of it as a prison and part as a home for disabled soldiers from their small army. In 1866, following the Austro-Prussian War in which the Duchy of Nassau had allied with the losing side, the castle was taken over by the Prussians.

The crown prince, Frederick Wilhelm, fell in love with the castle, but did little to prevent its decline. In 1900, with the help of Kaiser Wilhelm II, Marksburg was finally purchased by the German Castles Association for the symbolic sum of 1,000 gold marks (about 12,000 US dollars), and the association set up its headquarters there. Architect Bodo Ebhard, who had promoted the purchase, was commissioned to restore the castle's 15th-century appearance. (G.G.)

Marksburg has a triangular ground plan distinctive of the period of the Swabian dynasty. The three asymmetrical wings of the complex are set around a courtyard, which is also triangular. The southern wing, the one most exposed to attacks, is protected by the *Kaiser Heinrich Tower* (inside which is the chapel

that, in 1437, was consecrated to Saint Mark, after whom the fortress was named) whereas the east wing features the magnificent *pfalz* with the Knights' Hall. The structure known as the *Rheinebau* is located in the center. In 1283, the counts of Katzenelnbogen modified the heart of the castle, giving it its current stark Gothic appearance. The first line of defensive structures was added during the following century. In 1429, Marksburg was taken over by the counts of Hesse, who adapted it to accommodate artillery and added the ramparts with round towers. It was restored in the early 19th century based on drawings done by Wilhelm Dilich in about 1607. The 132-foot-high keep was originally crowned by a 26-foot round tower that was demolished in March 1945. (G.R.)

132-133 *Standing in the forest overlooking the city on the banks of the Neckar, the magnificent ruins of Heidelberg Castle forlornly evoke the misfortunes of the Palatinate, which was devastated by a series of ruthless military campaigns.*

133 top *The Ottheinrichsbau is the highlight of the complex. Prince Elector Otto Heinrich built it between 1556 and 1559, and it is* considered a masterpiece of the German Renaissance. The entrance, by Flemish maste, Alexander Colyn of Mechelen, is superb.*

133 bottom *The Deutsches Apotheken Museum, located in the Ottheinrichsbau, is a pharmacy museum full of precious pottery, 18th-century furniture, and instruments used to make ancient recipes.*

Heidelberg

GERMANY

According to local legend, in ancient times a witch named Jetta lived on the hill of Jettenbühel, which towered over the left bank of the Neckar. She ruled over the animals in the forest and the nymphs in the river. However, history tells us that the Count Palatine Conrad – this title was bestowed on him by his brother, Emperor Frederick Barbarossa – built his residence on this hill in 1155. As a result, the town of Heidelberg, which developed at the foot of the castle, became the capital of the Rhenish Palatinate. It expanded and grew rich, founding Germany's first university as well as an extensive and labyrinthine castle that romantics dubbed "the German Alhambra." Indeed, like the Alhambra in Granada, this mosaic of palaces and towers is an empty, abandoned shell. It took three centuries to build its marvelous array of Gothic, Renaissance, and Baroque buildings, and it took only three attacks – two human and one divine – to destroy it.

The Palatine Prince Elector Ruprecht III (1398-1410) started construction in about 1400, and his successors continued to enlarge and embellish the castle. Between 1556 and 1559, Otto Heinrich built a palace that was a masterpiece of the German Renaissance. Frederick V – the unfortunate "winter king," so called because he wore the Bohemian crown for just a few months before he was defeated and driven from Prague – had extensive excavation work done to create an enormous Italian garden with terracing. He also had the charming Elisabethentor built in just one night: this small triumphal arch was a tribute to his consort Elizabeth Stuart, a royal surprise from a prince in love. However, Frederick V was also the one who led Heidelberg and its magnificent castle into the horrors of war. During the Thirty Years War (1618-48), the city was devastated in 1622, and then again in 1633 and 1635. Nevertheless, the worst was yet to come. In 1689, French troops led by General Melac, "the incendiary of Louis XIV," bombarded Heidelberg and then entered the town, sacking it and burning all its buildings, including the castle. Only one house escaped destruction.

Heidelberg was rebuilt but four years later it was razed once more, again by the French, as Louis XIV had ordered his army to turn the Palatinate into a desert. Lastly, on June 23, 1764, the night before Prince Elector Karl Theodore was to move back into the castle after restoring part of the residence, as workers were carrying in the last pieces of furniture, lightning struck the octagonal tower, setting the beams on fire and dealing a final blow to the castle. Ever since then it has been abandoned to its ghosts: the pale wife of a Frankish duke who sits by the castle's pointed windows, wearing her crown; two black knights who walk back and forth across the castle's inaccessible rooftops; hunchbacked musicians playing diabolical airs in the chapel; the White Lady who passes beneath the vaults, prophesying the misfortunes of the Palatinate. (G.G.)

The ruins of Heidelberg castle, which can easily be considered the most superb castle, and the most eloquent blend of the art of construction of the German Middle Ages, Renaissance and Baroque, look like a long line of crimson walls. There is no true uniformity here. The massive and imposing ruins roughly consist of a quadrilateral complex with round towers and a courtyard with buildings from various eras set around it. Gothic structures predominate in the western and southern parts, whereas the northern and eastern ones boast the tall magnificent walls of the *Otto-Heinrichsbau*, with a superb Italian façade decorated with caryatids. This structure is considered a masterpiece of the German Renaissance. Prince Elector Ruprecht III (1398-1410) built the first fortified residence (*Ruprechtsbau*), which his successors transformed into a palace, adding the *Friedrichsbau* (1601-7) designed by Johann Schoch, and the *Englischerbau*. The entire complex was destroyed during the Thirty Years War. Reconstructed by Prince Karl Ludwig (1649-1680), it was devastated a short time later by the French. Reconstructed yet again, it was subsequently abandoned and used as a quarry for a ready supply of stones. Count Graimberg put an end to this destruction. Today, these well-maintained ruins represent one of Germany's most visited monuments. The castle is famous for the four granite columns from a Carolingian residence, the Pharmacy Museum, and the famous *Grosses Fass*, a 55,000-gallon barrel made in 1751 from the wood of over 100 oak trees. (G.R.)

134 *Eltz castle, emerging dramatically from the dark valley of Elzbach, is composed of an enormous tower whose compact form, animated by projections, is crowned by half-timbered towers.*

Eltz
GERMANY

The imposing castle of Eltz is perched atop a rocky hill that towers over a dark valley along the Rhine, near Koblenz. Its history begins in the 9th century with simple earthworks and a palisade. Stone eventually replaced the earth and wood structures. By 1157, during the period of Emperor Frederick Barbarossa (1152-90), the fortress of Eltz had become an important stronghold regulating the trade route between the Moselle Valley and the Eifel region. The castle was named after the Eltz River that flows past the rocky hill on which it was built, and its lords, in turn, took their name from the stronghold. The castle later became the undivided property of the three branches of the Eltz family, the Rodendorf, Rübenach, and Kempenich lines. Their descendants – several hundred – lived with their servants, guards, and farmers in the various buildings forming the complex. Eltz was gradually transformed into what the Germans referred to as a *Randhausburg*, or "castle-village." In the meantime, between 1470 and 1540, other wings and annexes were added to the original structures, transforming the fortress into the residence seen today.

During the 16th and 17th centuries, the members of the Eltz family held important positions in the Rhine region, particularly during the Wars of Religion between Catholics and Protestants. Some of them were elected prince-bishops of Trier and Mainz, and they played a significant role in imposing the Catholic Counter-Reformation. The castle was always their main center of power. In an unusual twist of events for a border area, Eltz survived the various conflicts that bloodied the region and marked the demise of many other castles. The only time the castle was seized was during the French Revolution, when the Jacobin armies occupied the Rhineland and set up a garrison at Eltz under French command at Koblenz. However, in 1815, Count Hugo Philipp zu Eltz regained control of the castle as its sole owner. His son, Count Karl, had it restored in a romantic style.

Construction lasted from 1845 to 1888 and cost an enormous amount of money. Fortunately, however, its original form was left untouched, unlike many of the imaginative "renovations" of the 19th century. (G.G.)

135 top *A round window bears the coat of arms of the Eltz-Kempenicher, one of the three branches of the family that owned the castle uninterruptedly until the late Middle Ages.*

135 bottom *Eltz is defined as a Randhausburg, or "castle-village." It was designed to house hundreds of people from different noble families, along with their servants.*

In the 19th century, Eltz was one of the favorite destinations of English travelers. In fact, Edward Murray's romantic guidebook, published in 1836, described it as a virtually unique example of a feudal residence that had eluded fire, war, and renovation. It was originally built in the 10th century, but the current *Randhausburg* (castle-village) dates back to the 12th century. The styles here range from the Romanesque to the Gothic and early Baroque. This impressive construction developed around an elongated oval courtyard, and the wings were connected to form a village: this was the fortified residence of the three branches of the Eltz family, a castle set 230 feet over the river (exactly the same height as the towers), on a rocky spur that influenced the layout of the floors and rooms. The castle is divided into "mansions" connected with the various

Eltz

branches of the family. The various rooms have been restored meticulously, and paintings and antique furniture are displayed.

The Rübenach mansion has weapons and antique armor, including Oriental armor, and a canopy bed from 1520. The nearby *Untersaal* boasts original Flemish tapestries, painted panels, and a *Madonna* by Lucas Cranach. The *Hall of the Electors Philipp Karl and Jakob* is located in the Rodendorf mansion, and tapestries from the Van der Brüggen workshop in Brussels are displayed here. The most lavish rooms are the *Knights' Hall*, with Gobelins works, and the *Hall of the Banners.* Everything here looks exactly as it did in 1490, and the *Schatzkammer* is still visible, with over 300 priceless late-medieval and Renaissance pieces (gold, porcelain, and sacred objects). (G.R.)

136-137 *The Rittersaal or Knights' Hall, which is now decorated with tapestries, 16th-century armor, and 17th-century furniture, was used for the parties, banquets, balls, and ceremonies that were an important part of the castellans' life.*

136 bottom *Next to the fireplace in the Prince Elector's room, there is an* enormous tapestry made in Brussels *in 1660 depicting animal scenes, which were very popular at the time.*

137 bottom *Nineteenth-century stained-glass windows and frescoes with late-Gothic motifs decorate the study. On the other hand, the writing desk and armchair are 17th-century originals.*

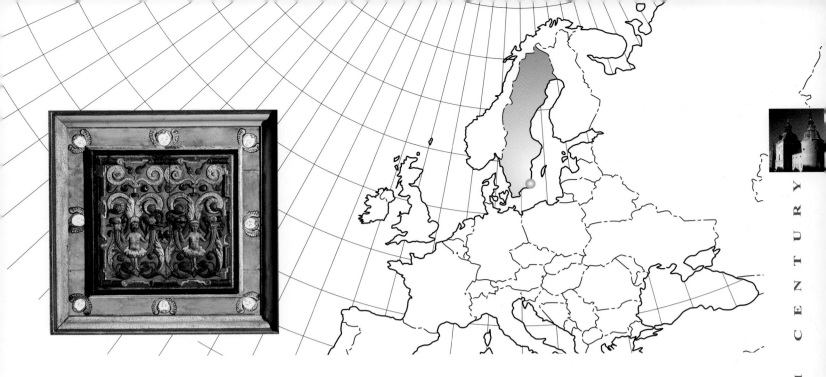

Kalmar

SWEDEN

The large and stately castle located in Sweden's oldest maritime city, founded on the Kalmar Sound across from the island of Öland and referred to as the "key to the kingdom" because of its strategic position, looks just as imposing as it did 500 years ago. It was initially a simple tower, built in the 12th century as a shelter and defense against the marauding pirates infesting the Baltic Sea. Important defensive structures were gradually added. At the time, the southern end of Sweden belonged to the kingdom of Denmark and the border was not far from Kalmar, which thus became the main fort protecting this frontier. It played this defensive role for several centuries and was besieged 24 times between 1307 and 1612. However, Kalmar was also a major port of call for the ships of the Hanseatic League, which dominated the Baltic and the North Sea.

One of the most memorable events in the history of Scandinavia took place at the castle in 1397. Delegates from the three Nordic kingdoms met here and signed the Union of Kalmar, uniting the crowns of Sweden, Norway, and Denmark under a single monarch, Eric VII (1412-39) of Pomerania, the grandson of Queen Margaret I (1387-1412) of Denmark. However, this union was not destined to last, and 150 years later Sweden proclaimed its independence. Kalmar thus resumed its role as a defensive outpost against Danish invaders.

During the second half of the 16th century, Erik XIV (1560-68) and John III (1568-1587) of the Vasa dynasty rebuilt the castle in a Renaissance style and furnished it sumptuously, making it their favorite residence. Charles XI, who ruled from 1673 to 1692, was the last Swedish king to live here. By this time, Kalmar was no longer a fortress but a magnificent royal residence. Denmark had lost all its territorial holdings in Sweden, which in turn expanded to its modern-day borders. The castle was later used as a royal distillery and then as a prison. It was finally renovated in the 19th century and transformed into a museum. (G.G.)

138 The reddish walls of Kalmar Castle, distinguished by its sinuous and distinctively Scandinavian rooftops, are reflected in the still waters of a narrow stretch of the Baltic. The castle is located on the island of Öland.

139 top The Golden Hall has a lovely wooden ceiling with carved and painted allegorical figures.

The hall, used by King Johan III for celebrations and banquets, was built in 1576, at the height of the Swedish Renaissance.

139 bottom The massive square and round towers were designed to accommodate artillery: before Kalmar was converted into a lavish royal residence, it was the most fortified stronghold in the kingdom of Sweden.

Kalmar

The influence of German architecture spread as far as Scandinavia, where in the 12th century monarchs and magnates began to construct castles. Its current appearance is attributable to renovations by Gustavus Vasa (1532-60), who added ramparts, curtains, and enormous, heavily fortified towers for artillery. The lovely round towers of the actual castle reflect French stylistic elements, although these distinctive, sinuously elongated roofs can also be seen at Saxon Moritzburg and throughout the Baltic area. Despite the fact that it was besieged more than 20 times and was later exploited for a variety of different uses (armory, granary, prison, museum), the interior has maintained much of its stately Gothic architecture. The *State Chamber*, with its intricate decorative woodwork, is beautifully preserved, and the *Golden Hall*, where John III held his banquets, reflects the glory of the past in its splendid carved and painted ceilings. The monumental well in the central courtyard has Germanic characteristics, whereas the one in the western courtyard stands a magnificent portal that looks like a tribute to the Colosseum, modeled after Roman structures, with double Doric and Corinthian columns along the sides. The royal coat of arms of the Vasa dynasty, which stands out in the center, seems to portray a vase but is actually a sheaf of wheat. (G.R.)

140-141 *All kinds of game are depicted along the upper frieze of the Hunting Salon, which boasts an intricately carved and gilded ceiling. On the right, the splayed window overlooks the sea.*

141 *The picture shows the stark white interior of the church, which has a barrel vault. Built in 1592, it is furnished with pieces donated by King Gustav Adolph at the turn of the 17th century.*

Rundale
LATVIA

142-143 *Set in a sprawling park and surrounded by trees, Rundale is a typical 18th-century aristocratic residence. It was inspired by the era's unsurpassable model of a noble palace: the Sun King's palace at Versailles.*

His name was Ernst Johann Bühren but he had people call him Biron, claiming that he was related to the great French family. In reality, his background was far less aristocratic, as he was the son of a lesser nobleman from Westphalia and the nephew of the footman of the Duke of Courland. In fact, it was in Courland – modern-day Latvia – that he began his extraordinary ascent to power. At Mitau, he became the advisor and then lover of Anna, widow of Duke Fredrick, ruler of Courland. When Anna, a hitherto minor Romanov, was proclaimed Empress of All the Russias in 1730, Bühren-Biron quickly became indispensable to her as more than just her lover. He relieved her of the burden of state affairs by ruling in her stead, satisfied her every whim, shared her unbridled passion for luxury, and watched over her safety, consigning anyone who threatened her to icy Siberia or the executioner's axe. Hated by all the other courtiers but widely feared because of his seemingly indisputable sway over Anna, the empress' favorite was rewarded with the title of Duke of Courland-Semigallia. Thus, he decided to build himself a palace worthy of his astonishing career. He chose Rundale as his site and hired the great architect Bartolomeo Francesco Rastrelli, who would later build the

143 Framed by the two pillars of the main entrance, each of which is decorated with two Ionic columns crowned by two sculpted lions, the façade is divided into three levels, with an array of windows and a triangular pediment.

142 bottom Two long wings extend from the internal façade to enclose the courtyard of honor. The stables and storage areas, arranged in an exedra layout, are located behind the courtyard.

Winter Palace at St. Petersburg. An army of workers began to construct the palace in 1736.

Biron's luck was not destined to last. When Czarina Anna Ivanovna died suddenly in 1740, the hated Biron was arrested and condemned to death. However, under Czarina Elizabeth (1741-62), his sentence was commuted to exile in Siberia. Rundale was confiscated and was left unfinished until Catherine II pardoned Biron when she came to the throne in 1762. Old and deprived of all his power, he returned to his homeland, living there for the rest of his life. The castle was then transferred to Count Zubov, who was close to Catherine II, and later by marriage, to the Shuvalov family, which owned it until 1920, when it reverted to the Republic of Latvia as part of the agrarian reforms of the period. During this period, an elementary school was set up in the palace. Rudale was converted into a museum in 1933. During World War II part of the palace was used as a granary but did not suffer any damage. Restoration work began in 1972 and is still underway. (G.G.)

144-145 Construction on the palace, designed by the architect Rastrelli, began in 1736. However, most of the interior was completed between 1765 and 1768, when Biron regained possession of the castle after being exiled in Siberia for over 20 years. The photograph shows the majestic staircase of honor.

144 bottom left Confiscated by the Republic of Latvia in 1920, Rundale was turned into a Historical Museum in 1933. Work to restore the castle began in 1972. This picture shows the duchess' bedroom, decorated with numerous paintings.

Rundale

144 bottom right The duke's bedroom ends with a deep alcove that holds a canopy bed and is closed off by draperies. Two enormous ceramic stoves are visible along the sides. Portraits of the Russian rulers hang on the walls.

145 top The formal halls occupy the main portion of the palace of Rundale. The enormous and dazzling White Hall, elegantly decorated with graceful Rococo stuccowork, was used for balls.

145 bottom The Oriental porcelain displayed in the Porcelain Room is enhanced by its highly original layout. These porcelains pieces are part of the palace's treasures.

Rundale

Rundale is not a fortified castle and instead resembles a boreal Versailles. In fact, it is considered the most magnificent royal palace in Latvia. It was built in the Baroque-Rococo style for the Duke of Courland, a veritable sovereign, and was designed by Italian architect Bartolomeo Francesco Rastrelli, who personally supervised the work. Francesco Martini and Carlo Zucchi followed the architect from St. Petersburg, frescoing the ceilings and walls, while the Berlin sculptor Johann Michael Graff displayed his entire repertoire of stuccowork here. The work on the palace brought the competition rampant among the monarchies of the 18th century to the Baltic: dazzling visitors with magnificent decorations. The palace was built around a central block, where the Throne Room, the White Room, and the Grand Gallery are located. The palace had nearly 140 rooms that were filled with artwork, but most of it has been lost. The entire complex was decorated with extraordinary luxury, with breathtaking boiserie, chandeliers, priceless parquet and marble. It was also surrounded by an extensive park with age-old trees. Rundale has now been converted into museum. (G.R.)

146 The ceiling in the Gold Ballroom is frescoed with figures of cherubs. The room is decorated with unusual stucco roses extending from the molding halfway down each panel.

146-147 The Gold Ballroom, with an enormous allegorical fresco on the ceiling and Bohemian crystal chandeliers, was the throne room of the Duchy of Courland-Semigallia during the brief period in which Ernst Johann Biron was in power.

147 bottom left Like any palace worthy of this name, Rundale also had a room used specifically for ducal audiences. The room, decorated entirely in red, boasted paintings by master artists.

147 bottom right Framed by the stucco decorations typical of the Rococo period, the fresco dominates the ceiling of the Audience Room.

The Kremlin
RUSSIA

During the Middle Ages, every Russian city had its own kremlin, or fortress. The word *kreml*, which may derive from the Tatar language, indicated a fortified area in which civil and religious authorities resided. Of all the extant kremlins, the one in Moscow is referred to as "the Kremlin," and it was the heart of Holy Russia under the czars and then of the Soviet Union. In 1156, Yuri Dolgoruki, the Prince of Suzdal, built a wooden fortress on the banks of the Moscow River, but the Tatars razed it in 1238 and the site remained deserted for a century. In 1326, another prince, Ivan Kalita, rebuilt Moscow and its kremlin, moving the metropolitan of

the Orthodox Church there from Vladimir and building the first stone churches behind wooden palisades. Fifty years later, these walls were replaced with lengthier stone walls and towers were added. Nevertheless, in 1382, the Tatars destroyed the city once again, killing half of the population.

The Kremlin was rebuilt for the third time under Ivan the Great III (1462-1505), who constructed the stronghold in its current size and layout. He commissioned Italian architects Aristotele Fioravanti, Pietro Antonio Solari, Marco Ruffo, and Aloisio da Milano to oversee the work. The architects rebuilt the walls and towers in brick, and working with local craftsmen they created a unique style that was imitated by other Russian cities. For the next 200 years, the Kremlin – to which other constructions were gradually added – was the residence of the czars. It was the stage of the dramas and tragedies of the Russian court: the rule of Ivan the Terrible,

148-149 The Great Palace, the Cathedral of the Annunciation, the Cathedral of the Archangel and the Ivan the Great Bell Tower rise above the red-brick walls dominated by the Tainitskaya Tower.

149 top In 1937, five synthetic ruby stars in gilded settings were installed on the five tallest towers. The stars, mounted on ball bearings, sway in the wind. The smallest one weighs over a ton.

149 center Twenty towers dot the curtain wall, the work of two Sforza architects, Pietro Antonio Solari and Marco Ruffo. The duo created a style that combined the stylistic elements of the Byzantine with those of the early Italian Renaissance.

149 bottom The stark skyscrapers of the Stalinist period tower over the Kremlin, which once dominated the city. Until the early 20th century, none of the buildings in Moscow were taller than three or four stories.

150-151 *The Cathedral of the Assumption or of the Dormition was built between 1475 and 1479 by the skilled Italian architect Aristotele Fioravanti, who successfully merged Russian traditions with the modern innovative techniques of the Italian Renaissance. The cathedral was designed to host coronation ceremonies and important masses.*

The Kremlin

150 bottom The Ivan the Great Bell-Tower is divided into two adjacent buildings: the 265-foot tower and another lower structure with an arch that houses the Czar Bell, weighing 220 tons and cast in the 18th century.

151 A masterpiece of Russian art, the Cathedral of the Annunciation was built in the late 14th century as a private chapel for the czar's family. The elegant cathedral with nine gilded domes is one of the oldest and most famous in Moscow, and it is the largest building inside the Kremlin.

the usurpation of Dmitri the Imposter, the conquest of the capital by the Polish army, the rise of the Romanov dynasty, and the massacre of the *streltsy*, the rebellious imperial guards that Peter I (later "the Great") had executed after their involvement with Princess Sophia, the regent, who opposed Peter's succession to the throne.

Several years later, Peter the Great moved his capital to St. Petersburg, the new city he had built on the shores of the Baltic. However, the Kremlin remained the religious center of the Russian empire and the patriarchs' residence. The czars spent a great deal of time here, building new palaces in the style of the period and repairing the damage caused by the numerous fires that ultimately destroyed the last of the Kremlin's wooden buildings.

In 1812, Napoleon took Moscow, and before abandoning the city he ordered his soldiers to demolish the Kremlin. However, only a few of the mines exploded, damaging various towers. Other buildings were added during the 19th century. During the Russian Revolution of November 1917, the Bolsheviks finally managed to seize the Kremlin after days of terrible fighting, and in March 1918 the Soviet government, headed by Lenin, moved into the stronghold, abandoning St. Petersburg as it was exposed to attacks. Several buildings in poor condition were torn down during the 1920s and 1930s whereas others were restored. The Palace of Congresses was built in 1961. (G.G.)

152-153 A decorated canopy
with faux ermine curtains crowns
the czar's throne (center) as well as
the thrones of the dowager empress
and the czarina (sides) in St.
Andrew Hall.

The Kremlin

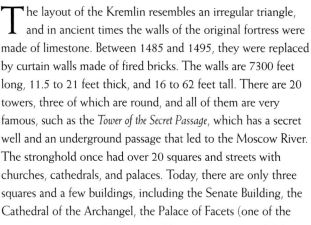

T he layout of the Kremlin resembles an irregular triangle, and in ancient times the walls of the original fortress were made of limestone. Between 1485 and 1495, they were replaced by curtain walls made of fired bricks. The walls are 7300 feet long, 11.5 to 21 feet thick, and 16 to 62 feet tall. There are 20 towers, three of which are round, and all of them are very famous, such as the *Tower of the Secret Passage*, which has a secret well and an underground passage that led to the Moscow River. The stronghold once had over 20 squares and streets with churches, cathedrals, and palaces. Today, there are only three squares and a few buildings, including the Senate Building, the Cathedral of the Archangel, the Palace of Facets (one of the

oldest buildings in Moscow, which was once used for the ceremonies and receptions of the czars), the Great Palace of the Kremlin, the Palace of Congresses, the Cathedral of the Assumption, the Church of the Deposition, the Cathedral of the Annunciation, the Patriarchs' Palace, Terem Palace (reserved for the czar's family; it is an extraordinary monument to the architecture and lifestyle of 17th-century Russia), and, above all, the State Armory, where the insignia of the imperial coronations are kept. These include the Monomakh Crown, the crown of Catherine II, studded with 5,000 diamonds, and the scepter with the enormous Orlov Diamond weighing nearly 200 carats. (G.R.)

152 bottom left *St. George Hall is one of the largest and most majestic in the palace. Eighteen pillars crowned with marble statues - allegorical representations of the lands and countries that formed the Russian state - support the vaulted ceiling decorated with stuccowork and rosettes.*

152 bottom right *The Great Palace was designed to exalt the grandeur of the monarchy and the stability of the Romanov line. It was built in neoclassical style with Baroque detailing, underscoring the pageantry and opulence of czarist Russia.*

153 *These two pictures show St. Alexander Hall (Alexandrovsky), next to St. Andrew Hall (Andreyevsky), built in honor of the Order of Alexander Nevsky,*

founded by Czarina Catherine I in 1725. Gilded chairs, with velvet upholstery and the star of the order attached to the back, are set along the pink marble walls.

The Kremlin

154 top Trefoil double-lancet windows and frescoes decorate the interior of a tower. Even the pavement is decorated with scenes. The towers were built by Italian architects between 1485 and 1508.

154 bottom Terem Palace, the czarinas' residence, was actually used by the czars as well. Its rooms, decorated with religious frescoes, were heated by enormous ceramic stoves.

154-155 The Palace of Facets, so called because of the ashlarwork of its façade, was built between 1487 and 1491 by Marco Ruffo and Pietro Antonio Solari. It was used to receive ambassadors, who were welcomed on the ground floor in this hall decorated with 17th-century frescoes.

155 bottom left Beyond the arched doorway decorated with gilded garlands, a beautiful ceramic stove heats the throne room of Terem Palace.

155 bottom right A Renaissance-style arch with a triangular pediment is the stately entrance to one of the rooms in the Palace of Facets.

156-157 *The Nogat formed a wide defensive barrier in front of the walls of Malbork, or ancient Marienburg. This was the residence of the Grand Master of the Teutonic Order, founded in the Holy Land to defend the Holy Sepulcher and then brought to Prussia to conquer pagan lands.*

156 bottom *Several buildings were constructed around the original nucleus of the actual castle. They were used for various purposes when Malbork became the small capital of a rich and powerful monastic state.*

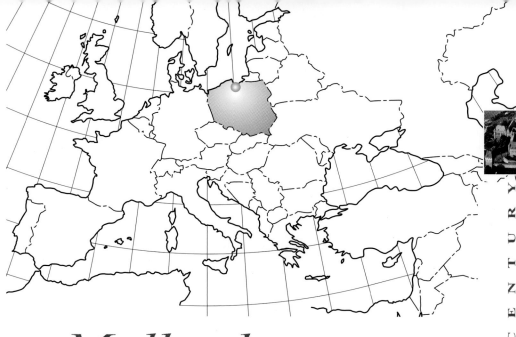

157 *The 14th-century Middle Castle, built around a vast rectangular courtyard, was the Palace of the Grand Masters. It included the private apartments and formal halls, all of which had magnificent vaulted ceilings.*

Malbork

POLAND

More than a castle – it is the largest one in Europe – Malbork, or ancient Marienburg, is a fortified town encircled by a double ring of walls and dotted with about 30 semicircular towers with pointed roofs. Its origins go back to the 13th century, when Conrad, the Duke of Mazovia, was unable to subdue the pagan tribes of the Borussians (after whom Prussia was named). As a result, he turned to the monastic-military Knights of the Teutonic Order, which had been founded in the Holy Land during the crusades to defend the Holy Sepulcher. As a reward for their assistance, these pious soldiers were given part of the territory they had conquered, and they established their small capital near Danzig (modern-day Gdansk), on the banks of the Nogat, a tributary of the Vistula. Marienburg, the residence of the Grand Master of the Order, was founded here in 1274. This majestic brick complex included the apartments of the knights and their guests, a monumental kitchen, stables, a brewery, a chapel, a chapter house, a bakery, prisons, and two refectories – a summer one and a winter one – that could accommodate hundreds of people. This was because the Order's policy was to offer lavish banquets to display all its wealth and power to princes and to the local tribal chieftains. The granaries used to store foodstuffs were enormous. These provisions were transported to Danzig, the Hanseatic trading center, and from the port they were then shipped to Germany. The sale of wheat grown in these conquered lands was the basis of the economy of the Teutonic Knights, who by the 15th century dominated a state extending from Prussia to Estonia. The kingdom of Prussia arose following secularization of the Order during the Protestant Reformation.

During the 14th century, architect Nikolaus Fellenstein reconstructed the buildings at Marienburg in the Gothic style. The town developed around it and was stoutly defended by new ramparts. In fact, when the Poles attacked the castle in 1410 after defeating the Order at the Battle of Tannenberg, they were ultimately forced to withdraw. However, in 1456 the impoverished Teutonic Knights were forced to hand the castle over to mercenaries in lieu of payment. These mercenaries, in turn, sold the castle to Casimir IV (1447-92), the Jagiellonian

king of Poland, who had it adapted as a residence for himself and his successors. With the partition of Poland in the 18th century, Marienburg went to the Prussians, who demolished part of it and converted the rest into barracks. Restoration work began in 1817. (G.G.)

This immense complex is divided into three sectors: the *High Castle*, which corresponds to the oldest part; the *Middle Castle*, built in the 14th century; and the *Low Castle*, which was originally used as a defensive outpost beyond the walls of the stronghold. A wide fortified esplanade with the Gothic church of St. Lawrence (14th century) is all that remains of the latter. In the *Middle Castle* – the Palace of the Grand Masters – the apartments of the Grand Master, with magnificent vaulted rooms, are extraordinary. The kings of Poland later turned the Middle Castle into a royal residence. The *High Castle*, an impressive quadrangular structure with extremely tall roofs, is composed of rooms boasting magnificent architectural features and sculptures: chapels, the chapter house, the treasury, the refectory, the knights' dormitories, kitchens, cells, and an infirmary. Today most of them house the museum's collections of medieval artifacts, weapons and armor, furniture, and a superb collection of amber masterpieces. The church dedicated to Our Lady was exquisite and had a Gothic *Golden Door* with the polychrome decorative motifs distinctive of the Middle Ages. (G.R.)

Karlstejn

CZECH REPUBLIC

158-159 Karlstejn looks like a compact block of buildings dominated by the squat tower of the treasury. Crenellated walls encircle the entire complex.

158 bottom The Chapel of St. Catherine, whose walls are encrusted with gemstones, was the private oratory of King Charles IV, who would retire here to meditate and ponder his political decisions.

Like all the monarchs of medieval Europe, who were sovereigns through the grace of God, Charles IV of Luxembourg (1346-78), King of Bohemia and Holy Roman Emperor, was a great collector of relics. The sacred remnants ensuring God's favor were jealously guarded and stored in dazzling anthropomorphic reliquaries, masterpieces crafted in gold and gemstones. To protect this spiritual treasure, which was also worth an unimaginable amount of money, Charles IV had a special castle constructed. This invincible stone treasury was built about 18 miles from his capital city, Prague, on a site amid craggy ramparts surrounded by ravines. The first stone was laid on June 10, 1348 and was

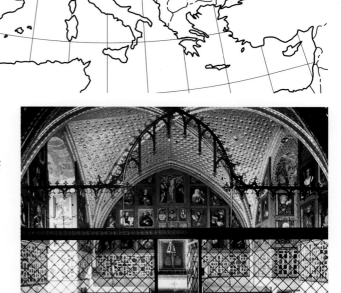

159 The crown jewels and priceless relics were kept in the Chapel of the Holy Cross. Over 2,200 gems are set in the walls, which have 128 panels with figures of saints and angels. The insignias of the Holy Roman Empire and of the Kingdom of Bohemia are preserved behind the altar.

blessed by Archbishop Arnost of Pardubice (this ecclesiastical participation was unusual, because it consecrated a military structure that would also house sacred relics). Construction, headed by French architect Matthias of Arras and Bohemian Peter Parler, was not completed until 1367, although enough of it had been finished by 1355 to allow King Charles to live there. Indeed, the king could live there but not the queen. The castle's religious use gave it an almost monastic character and women were not allowed to sleep there. For his consort, Charles thus had another castle – Karlík – built not far from Karlstejn, as a place where he could enjoy the pleasures of conjugal and courtly life. The king and emperor also had the imperial jewels brought to Karlstejn. The jewels, which were also considered sacred, were transported to Prague every year to celebrate the anniversary of Charles' coronation and be displayed to his subjects. The castle and its treasures were guarded by a burgrave assisted by 22 knights and 20 vassals. Ten of them remained on guard day and night, keeping watch from the towers. Every hour, "in a loud and clear voice" they had to cry out "Away from here! Away from these walls! Do not approach or you will die!" to frighten off any thieves hiding in the woods around the fortress.

The priceless relics were safeguarded in the best-protected part of the castle, the Chapel of the Holy Cross. The chapel, located in the donjon, was protected by four iron gates, each of which had 19 locks. The treasure was also protected by the painting of a group of saints, the work of court artist Master Theodoricus. Only the archbishops could celebrate Mass here, and the king himself had to take off his shoes before entering. The chronicler of Charles IV proudly wrote, "There does not exist a more beautiful chapel anywhere in the world."

However, Charles' son and successor, Wenceslas IV, was the last sovereign to live in the castle, which the Hussite rebels besieged unsuccessfully for six months in 1422. The imperial jewels were transported to Nuremberg, while the Bohemian crown jewels and the royal archives were transferred to Prague in 1619, followed by the relics. The castle fell into ruin and was assigned to the queens, but it was used only as a warehouse and granary until 1886, when it was completely restored by architect Josef Mocker, who gave it its current appearance. (G.G.)

The layout of Karlstejn Castle is oddly elongated and its fixed ascending path reflected the heavenly ascent, passing through the Vorsilska Tower, the Burgrave's Court, the Well Tower, and the Imperial Palace. An outside staircase led to the Hall of the Vassals. The imperial apartment, with the chapel with the triptych of *The Madonna with Child*, is on the upper floor. This floor also had a hall where a 14th-century painter known only as the "Master of the Family Tree" completed a famous set of portraits of the ancestors of Charles IV. These paintings have since been lost. Other apartments were located on the third floor, and the diptych by Tommaso da Modena can still be seen in one of the bedrooms. Mary's Tower houses the Church of Our Lady, whose walls and ceiling are covered with frescoes attributed to Nicholas Wurmser, and the extraordinary Chapel of St. Catherine, whose walls are encrusted with gems and semiprecious stones. This is where Charles would come to meditate and make political decisions.

A drawbridge led to the Great Tower, which was 121 feet tall and had walls that were 20 feet thick. It houses one of the most spectacular rooms in Europe, comparable only to the Scrovegni Chapel frescoed by Giotto. This is the Chapel of the Holy Cross, where the most sacred treasures of the empire were safeguarded behind four doors with 19 locks. The chapel's Gothic vault was covered entirely with decorated stuccowork and Venetian glass depicting the sun, moon, and stars. The lower band of the walls is covered with gilded stuccowork set with thousands of stones. Above this are 129 splendid Gothic panels painted by Master Theoderik (14th century) depicting Christ's heavenly army. The chapel symbolized Celestial Jerusalem and was illuminated by 1,300 candles. (G.R.)

160 Nothing remains of the original medieval castle of Hluboká, nor of the Renaissance residence that was built over it. The modern building discordantly resembles a Tudor castle and was in fact modeled after Windsor.

Hluboká
CZECH REPUBLIC

160-161 The Vtlava River meanders lazily near the white complex, which has 144 rooms full of antique furniture, tapestries, porcelain pieces, and hunting trophies. The paintings alone number nearly 1,000.

Schwarzenberg Königreich, the Schwarzenberg Kingdom: the name given to a group of fiefdoms in southern Bohemia carried no irony but a touch of deferential consternation inspired by the power of one of the wealthiest families of the Hapsburg Empire. The kingdom had more than 440,000 acres of fields, meadows, forests, and marshes abounding with game. It was dotted with country houses and hunting lodges, and was home to 230,000 hardworking subjects. Like any true kingdom, it naturally had a small army: a private guard corps with several hundred grenadiers dressed in light-blue pants and white jackets – these were the colors of the House of Schwartzenberg – and wearing dazzling gilded helmets decorated with rooster feathers. These soldiers first assembled in 1705 in the courtyard of the

161 bottom An extraordinarily intricate handle depicts a falcon plucking the eye from a mustached janissary, evoking the exploits of Adolf zu Schwarzenberg, who defeated the Turks at Raab in 1589.

castle of Hluboká, which was the tiny capital of this vast dominion at the time and was later replaced by the more imposing Krumlov.

The Schwarzenbergs, a noble German family from Lower Franconia, came to Bohemia in 1660 when Johann Adolph I (1615-1683) purchased the fief of Trebon. In 1661, he purchased Hluboká, a stronghold built on a hill near the Vltava River during the era of King Wenceslas I (1230-53). The castle was later renovated several times to cater to changing tastes. Johann Adolph's son, Franz Adam, inherited both Hluboká and Krumlov in 1719, effectively establishing the Schwarzenberg Kingdom and becoming its first sovereign. An energetic and brilliant administrator, the perfect courtier, a generous benefactor, and above all, a

162 top *The Gothic arches of two galleries frame the double staircase of honor. The galleries display portraits of the ancestors of the Schwarzenbergs, one of the most affluent and powerful families in the Hapsburg Empire.*

162-163 *The well-lit library, which boasts a carved and gilded Baroque ceiling, is filled with books as well as 17th- and 18th-century globes.*

Hluboká

163 left An elaborate Murano-glass chandelier hangs from the vault of the Great Room. A painting by Jan Brueghel the Younger hangs behind the collection of Delft ceramics decorating the Baroque fireplace.

163 right The Great Room is decorated with period furniture, and 18th-century family portraits hang amidst the Rococo boiseries.

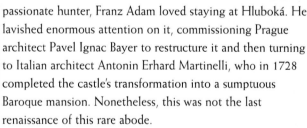

passionate hunter, Franz Adam loved staying at Hluboká. He lavished enormous attention on it, commissioning Prague architect Pavel Ignac Bayer to restructure it and then turning to Italian architect Antonin Erhard Martinelli, who in 1728 completed the castle's transformation into a sumptuous Baroque mansion. Nonetheless, this was not the last renaissance of this rare abode.

In the first half of the 19th century, the Austrian aristocracy became enamored of all things English. While his peers merely surrounded their country residences with vast English-style parks and installed tennis courts between their stables and fish ponds, Johann Adolph II – the new ruler of the Schwarzenberg Kingdom and the brother of Felix, prime minister of the Hapsburg Empire, and of Friedrich, cardinal of Salzburg and then of Prague – went overboard. He and his wife Eleanor, who was born in Liechtenstein, had made many trips to England, culminating in 1838 when they attended the celebrations for the coronation of Queen Victoria. During their visits, the two – who shared the same tastes – never tired of seeing Windsor Castle, as they were enchanted with its Tudor style. In fact, when they returned to their homeland they decided to give southern Bohemia an incongruous and very British mansion whose ethereal appearance in the heart of the Czech forest is like a startling specter out of place and time. (G.G.)

This white residence has an elongated layout and is flanked by a series of elegant Tudor-style towers set in the main body. There are 140 rooms, one-third of which are open to the public, and over 40,000 works of art are displayed here. There are 900 paintings, including *The Twelve Months*, eleven hunting scenes by Snyders, and five landscapes by John George Hamilton, as well as 57 Flemish tapestries from the 16th century, antique and modern furniture, Saxon silver, Oriental antiques, racks with steel weapons and firearms, Bohemian crystal, and ceramics from Faenza. The rooms include the dining hall, which boasts a Renaissance coffered ceiling from the castle of Cesky Krumlov (Krummau), the marble hall, the weapons room with statues of Adolph zu Schwarzenberg (who defeated the Turks at Raab in 1598) and Karl zu Schwarzenberg (who fought at the Battle of Leipzig in 1813), the reading room, and the theater. The library is extraordinary: it boasts lavish bookcases from the late Baroque period that the family brought here from its castle at Scheinfeld, in Bavaria, and it has over 12,000 exquisitely bound books. A Baroque sled and a coach from 1638, which belonged to the Eggenberg family, formerly the lords of Cesky Krumlov, are displayed in one of the hallways. (G.R.)

164-165 *The road that zigzags up to the fortress is fortified by 14 gates: getting past them all would have been an arduous undertaking for attackers.*

164 bottom *Strategically positioned like an eagle's nest, Hochosterwitz was designed to barricade the road to Carinthia. As the danger of Turkish invasions waned, however, the castle was converted into an aristocratic residence.*

165 top *A line of 16th-century armor seems to pay tribute to the Khevenhüllers, the smiling castellans portrayed in the 18th-century portrait on the wall.*

Hochosterwitz

AUSTRIA

Hochosterwitz fortress, built atop a rocky spur in Carinthia and towering over the surrounding plains, dates back to about 860, when Austria was a march, or borderland. It was a bastion of the Holy Roman Empire overlooking the Pannonian lands that were wide open to invaders, from the Avars to the Slavs and the Hungars. Its castellans, the Osterwitzer, were the watchful guardians of those threatened border areas, and in 1209 Otto IV granted them the title of Great Imperial Cupbearers. They bravely defended the march until 1475, when the latest conquerors arriving from Asia, the Turks, vanquished the fortress in a sudden, devastating raid and captured the last Osterwitzer, who died in prison. Since the family died out with him, the castle reverted to Emperor Frederick III (1440-93), who assigned a garrison to it that valiantly fought off other attacks by the Turks. A century later, Ferdinand I (1558-64) entrusted it to the capable leadership of Christof Khevenhüller, provincial captain of Carinthia. However, it was his son Georg who purchased it and made it the family's key holding. Georg also fortified the castle further to protect it from the growing Turkish threat. After seizing Hungary, the Turkish sultan seemed intent on conquering Austria.

A great lord, intelligent benefactor, and skilled soldier, Georg Khevenhüller transformed Hochosterwitz into what it is today a princely Italianate residence while also attempting to make it invincible. He reinforced its defenses by building 14 fortified gates to block the impassable access route that winds its way up the mountain. This concept, unique in the history of castle architecture, is also a minor masterpiece of architectural Mannerism. The work was completed 15 years later, in 1586, and Baron Georg was so proud of the outcome that he had a marble tablet mounted on one of the walls in the courtyard of the castle, expressing the wish that his descendants would always retain possession of the structure and maintain it with the same passion he had dedicated to his creation. His wish was fulfilled: his descendants still own Hochosterwitz, which has always been the residence of the main branch of the Khevenhüller family. (G.G.)

The tall hill with the castle barricaded the Zollfeld, the "bulwark of Christianity" that had to be defended at all cost. The layout is simple: a rectangular castle-palace on a hilltop with three round towers at its corners.

To reach it, however, one has to get past three moats and 14 fortified gates: *Fähnrichtor, Wächtertor, Nautor, Engelstor, Löwentor, Manntor, Khevenhüllertor, Landschafstor, Reisertor, Waffentor, Mauertor, Brückentor, Kulmentor,* and *Kirchentor.*

Each gate is more impressive and splendid than the last. They are veritable triumphal arches symbolizing Hochosterwitz's fame as an impregnable fortress.

Its rooms now hold collections of paintings, prehistoric artifacts, weapons, and armor, including one set of armor that is over eight feet tall. As legend would have it, during a siege, its owner terrified the Turks, putting them to flight simply by declaring that he was the shortest of his comrades. (G.R.)

166 The mighty turreted fortress crowns the highest portion of the Mönchsberg and is the most distinctive feature of the Salzburg landscape.

167 The prince-archbishops of Salzburg often retreated to Hohensalzburg, their official residence, when their heavy-handed worldly rule sparked the rage - and rebellion - of their subjects.

Festung Hohensalzburg
AUSTRIA

Before becoming famous among music lovers around the world as the city of Mozart, Salzburg boasted another title: the "German Rome," as it was the religious capital of Catholic Germany. In fact, the city was founded by a saint, Bishop Rupert of Worms, who built a monastery on the Mönchsberg (Monks' Hill) over the ruins of the Roman town of Juvavum, which was destroyed by the Huns. At the same time, his niece founded the Nonnberg Convent on the banks of the Salzach, and a town gradually developed between these two religious settlements. Rupert's successors ruled over the town, initially under the auspices of the dukes of Bavaria and then under the emperors, gradually expanding their power and holdings. In 784, Charlemagne made them archbishops, and in 1278, Rudolph of Hapsburg made them princes of the Holy Roman Empire. Indeed, they always acted more like princes than like men of the Church.

In 1077, Gebhard built the fortress of Hohensalzburg on another steep hill, making it the archbishop's residence. Construction continued and the fortress was enlarged until it ultimately became one of the most imposing military complexes in Central Europe. The archbishops sought refuge here during troubled periods, for example from 1520 to 1526, during the Peasants' War that shook Germany, already inflamed by Martin Luther's religious rebellion. These ecclesiastical princes were heavy-handed with their subjects, preferring the sword to the crosier. Leonhard von Keutschach put the city's notables in chains because they insisted that they would only take orders from the emperor, and in 1511, he was forced to lock himself up in Hohensalzburg to flee the angry uprising of Salzburg's oppressed citizens. Leonhard was the one who transformed the castle into a lavish Renaissance residence.

The most intriguing of these harsh prelates was Wolf Dietrich von Raitenau, who loved to refer to himself as *Archiepiscopus et Princeps*. Elected in 1587 by the canons of the cathedral when he was just 28 years old, he was "a religiously worldly archbishop." He loved art, literature and music (he founded the Salzburger Hofkapelle in 1591) and transformed the diocese into a court. Lavish as it was, Hohensalzburg was inadequate for him, and he began to renew the city, adding constructions in the new Counter-Reformation style that was spreading across Catholic Europe from Rome. He built the Residenz for himself and Mirabell Palace for his beautiful lover, Salome Alt. He rebuilt the old Romanesque cathedral that had been destroyed by fire. According to legend, he was the one who set the fire – an ecclesiastical Nero – because he could no longer stand celebrating Mass in that "antique." Nevertheless, fate was cruel to Wolf Dietrich. He had abandoned the uncomfortable Hohensalzburg fortress to live in his new and luxurious Residenz in the heart of the city. After reigning for 24 years, however, in 1611 he was captured and imprisoned by Duke Maximilian of Bavaria, with whom he had had bitter territorial disagreements. A papal nuncio had the duke hand the prisoner over to him, but Wolf Dietrich was nonetheless forced to resign. His successor, Markus Sittikus von Hohenems, had the deposed archbishop locked up at Hohensalzburg, the fortress he so detested. He was held there for seven years, and after pining away with sadness and regret, he finally died of a broken heart in 1617. (G.G.)

The oldest part is the central portion known as the "Old Castle." It was reconstructed in the 15th century, when the round towers of the external curtain walls were also built. Archbishop Leonhard von Keutschach (1495-1519) enlarged it considerably, turning it into a fortified citadel rising on top of the Mönschberg. The external bastions were added in the 16th-17th centuries to ward off the threat of Turkish invasions. The residential quarters were renovated to be opulent but solemn rooms. One example is the famous Golden Hall, with twisted columns made of red marble, precious ceilings, intricate Gothic decorations and a famous majolica stove, a spectacular example of late medieval artwork that is exquisitely adorned with figures of the saints. The fortress, which has an extensive art collection, is easy to reach via a funicular installed in 1892. (G.R.)

Festung Hohensalzburg

168 Viewed from the park of Schloss Mirabell, the prince-bishops' Baroque summer palace, the pale fortress of Hohensalzburg stands out starkly beyond the cathedral, dwarfing it.

169 top The intricate decoration of one of the doors exemplifies the opulence of the private apartments of the prince-bishops, who lived here until the 17th century.

169 bottom The lower floors of Hohensalzburg house the Burgmuseum, which boast medieval paintings and sculptures, and a collection of weapons and armor, some of which seem ready for battle.

170 top Rosenburg Castle, perched on a rocky promontory towering over the Kamp River, was remodeled during the 16th and 17th centuries, transforming this sturdy medieval structure into a splendid country residence.

170-171 *From the balconies and covered roof-terraces of the towers, guests could watch jousts held on the grassy esplanade - the largest in Europe - surrounded by arches.*

Rosenburg
AUSTRIA

Toward the fateful year 1000, Lower Austria, which extended northward on the left bank of the Danube, was still an unconquered land across the river that, for centuries, had marked the boundary between two worlds: that of the Romans and that of the barbarians. This intricate maze of mountain chains and valleys was known as the land of Pforten, the "Gates" through which populations migrated and wealthy commercial traffic flowed. These included the Viennese, Hungarian, Moravian, and Bohemian gates. During these years of fighting, the gates had to be guarded constantly and barricaded when necessary. As a result, fortified castles were built on high ground and in the valleys. One of them was Rosenburg, which towered over the Kamp River: anyone marching on Vienna from Bohemia had to get past this stronghold. This long-feared event did not occur until 400 years after the fortress was built, when the belligerent Hussite heretics poured out of Bohemia, intent on destroying the Catholic Church, accused of being led by the Antichrist. Rosenburg was captured and devastated in 1433.

What remained of it, with its surrounding fief, was purchased in 1476 by Kaspar von Rogendorf, chamberlain of Emperor Frederick III (1440-93), who rebuilt the castle and then sold it to Jakob and Christoph Grabner in 1487. The Grabner brothers, followed by their children and grandchildren – Sebastian in particular – transformed Rosenburg from a medieval castle into a fortified noble residence built in the Renaissance style. From 1593 to 1597, Sebastian spent an enormous amount of money to "update" what had now become the family residence. Sebastian went heavily into debt and shortly thereafter his beloved wife died. As a result, he was forced to give up his dream and sell the castle. Hans Jörger von Tollet purchased it in 1604, but in 1611 he sold it to Cardinal Franz von Dietrichstein, who was Bishop of Olomuc at the time. The prelate's first move was to convert the castle chapel – designed for Protestant services, as this was the predominant faith in the area – into a Catholic church. A few years later, the Kamp River valley became the stage for the first battles of the Thirty Years War (1618-1648) pitting Catholics against Protestants, a war that would bathe all of Germany in blood. The Protestant military leader Freiherr von Hofkirchen captured Rosenburg Castle in 1620 and slaughtered all its defenders. Just half a century later, the fortress was a luxurious, aristocratic residence once more. Taken over by the Hoyos family, it was restored and embellished. At the same time, it lost its military importance when the Hapsburgs reconquered Hungary, eliminating all possible danger as the boundary thus shifted much farther south. (G.G.)

172 Portraits of family members hang on the walls of the Marble Hall, so called because of its marble floors. The room's vaulted ceiling is decorated with stuccowork.

172-173 Baroque bookcases with carved columns, each of which holds a marble or terracotta bust of a historic figure or deity, are aligned along the walls of the library and set between enormous windows. The library has a coffered ceiling.

The old medieval castle was built around a keep with a pentagonal courtyard and tall curtain walls. During the 16th and 17th centuries, it was enlarged and transformed into a lavish and picturesque Renaissance residence with the largest (223 x 151 feet) and currently best-preserved jousting court in Europe. A bird's-eye view reveals that the area with the turreted buildings is tiny in relation to the two enormous green courtyards (one of which is completely porticoed and looks like some of the Carthusian monasteries in Italy). The customary neo-Gothic renovations date to the 19th century. The castle's numerous opulently decorated rooms (notably the library, the chapel, and the music room) house interesting collections of paintings, artwork, priceless furniture, monumental stoves, steel weapons and firearms, and prehistoric artifacts collected by Baron Ferdinand von Engelshofen. (G.R.)

173 bottom One of the sitting
rooms, which has a coffered
ceiling, is decorated with 17th-
century furniture and still-lifes.

Rosenburg

174-175 Built on a cliff jutting
into Lake Geneva, Chillon Castle
was in a key strategic position,
controlling what was the main
route between Italy and Northern
Europe during the Middle Ages.

174 bottom The central square
tower is surrounded by walls with
abutting buildings. Other towers
are set along the lake, rising
impressively over the road skirting
the foot of the mountain.

Chillon

SWITZERLAND

Built on a rocky promontory jutting into Lake Geneva, the spectacular castle of Chillon seems to float on water. Its construction date is unknown, but it was first mentioned in documents in 1150. Its purpose was to control the road from Burgundy to the Great St. Bernard Pass, thus blocking the narrow route between the mountains and the lake. A Savoy fortress at the time, it was rebuilt and enlarged in 1248 by Peter of Savoy, known as "Le Petit Charlemagne," whose victory over the imperial troops helped him gain possession of the Vaud. Because of its charming position, during the following century it became the favorite summer residence of the Savoys and their court. During the Wars of Religion in the 16th century, the dukes of Savoy used it to house their prisoners. The most famous of them was François de Bonnivard, prior of St. Victor in Geneva and defender of his homeland against the Savoys, whose story was romanticized by Lord Byron's poem *The Prisoner of*

Chillon. Captured in the Jura Mountains by a group of bandits, Bonnivard was literally sold to the duke of Savoy, who locked him in his dungeon. For six years he was kept chained to a pillar, pacing around it like a caged animal. The ring fastening the chain to his waist and the rut hollowed in the stone floor by his footsteps are still visible. In 1536 an avenging fleet from Geneva, backed by Bernese troops, besieged and captured the castle, finally rescuing its prisoner.

Chillon was the residence of a Bernese bailiff until 1733, when it was transformed into a state prison. The cells that had once held the House of Savoy's enemies were thus used to incarcerate the propagandists of new and revolutionary ideas unacceptable to the *ancien régime*. Following the French occupation of Switzerland in 1798, the castle was used exclusively as a depot for weapons and munitions. (G.G.)

175 top The imposing round towers formed an obstacle preventing the transit of any hostile army that dared to venture into the narrow space between the mountain and the lake.

175 bottom Large windows covered with odd dormers overlooking the internal courtyard, which housed the stables, the storerooms, and the gatehouse.

An outpost was first built by the ancient Romans in a highly strategic position on a spur by the waterfront, in order to guard a narrow path cut between the mountains and the lake. In fact, together with the Great St. Bernard Pass, the "Chillon road" would later become known as the *Route d'Italie* – the road to Italy – because, for centuries, it was the only road connecting Italy and Northern Europe. A new fortress was built during the 11th century. During the 12th century, it was taken over by the counts of Savoy, who made it their residence and collected tolls here. The Savoyard counts were also the ones who gave Chillon its current appearance: a fortress on the side facing land but also a palace rising from the lake. This unique and intriguing complex is composed of approximately 25 different *corps de bâtiment*. The *Camera Domini*, the chapel, the great halls and the internal courtyards date to the Savoy period. Chillon had its own fleet at Lake Léman, the French name of Lake Geneva. The ships were built by Genoese carpenters. Increased use of the St. Gotthard Pass marked the decline of the *Route d'Italie* and of Chillon's importance as a military fortress. As a result, the castle was used as a prison. Chillon is one of the best-preserved medieval castles in Europe, and it has collections of artwork, ancient weapons, chests, artifacts discovered during excavations, and furniture. The château hosts numerous temporary exhibitions and cultural events. (G.R.)

176 Part of the castle was dug directly into the rock face, like this Gothic gallery with two aisles: its right wall is actually the side of the mountain.

Chillon

176-177 *Viewed from the lake, the castle is an impressive sight. The Savoys transformed this side of the complex into a delightful palace. From here, they would go boating and hunt aquatic birds.*

177 bottom *François de Bonnivard, a Protestant prior from Geneva, was the chateau's most famous prisoner: he was held in chains here for six years. He is depicted here in this lithograph of a painting by Eugène Delacroix.*

Chillon

178 The Savoy coat of arms decorates the large fireplace in this hall. Its coffered ceiling is supported by arches set on thick columns.

179 top left During the centuries of Savoy rule, the counts used the Hall of State, which has an ornate wooden ceiling, to meet with their advisors.

179 top right Some of the ancient defensive preparations have been preserved, such as this wooden staircase that led to the loopholes used by archers and crossbowmen to shoot their arrows.

179 bottom This large hall, displaying weapons, armor, and Baroque furniture, is in the hall overlooking the water. The Savoy apartments were located here.

Grandson

SWITZERLAND

180-181 The tall curtain walls of Grandson, lightened by elegant Gothic double-lancet windows in the area with the formal halls, have five towers with conical roofs, built between the 13th and 15th centuries.

The château was built on the shore of Lake Neuchâtel in the 11th century to block the coast road. It belonged to the Grandson family, which was one of the most illustrious in Switzerland. Several Grandsons became the bishops of Basel, Lausanne, Geneva, Toul, and Verdun, but the family died out in 1397 with Otto, who was killed in a judicial duel. Known as the "peerless knight," Otto courted the beautiful Catherine de Belp, the wife of Gerard d'Estavayer. In revenge, Gerard accused him of attempting to poison Amedeo Vili, the Count of Savoy. In keeping with medieval custom, the judgment of God would be proof of any misdeed. The two faced a fight to the death, armed with a lance, two swords, and a dagger. It was agreed that the vanquished would lose both hands unless he confessed: Otto to the crime of poisoning, Gerard to slander. Otto lost the duel and Gerard ordered him to confess. Otto responded by extending his hands, which Gerard severed with a single blow.

In 1476, Château Grandson was attacked by the enormous army led by Charles the Bold, the duke of

Burgundy, who was determined to subdue the Swiss. The besieged – approximately 800 people, including women, children, and the elderly – held out for 10 days. On the eleventh day, convinced by the pledge of clemency offered by one of the duke's envoys, they finally surrendered. As soon as they left the castle, however, the duke had them all killed, hanging hundreds of them from the trees near the castle or drowning them in the lake. Enraged by the news, the Swiss Confederate Army marched on Grandson, battling and routing the ducal army, despite the fact that the Burgundians had twice as many soldiers.

The Swiss attacked the castle so violently that the garrison immediately surrendered: the bodies of the Swiss, still hanging from the trees, were taken down in order to string up those of the Burgundians. The booty was immense. In addition to cannons, muskets, harquebuses, flags and silk-lined curtains, the Swiss also seized the duke's throne, gold and silver tableware, and 400 trunks full of precious fabrics.

180 bottom The courtyard of Grandson is virtually crushed by the wings enclosing it. The apartments added during the Renaissance are located in the center.

181 top The intricate 18th-century decorations on the

wrought-iron gate feature the heraldic emblems of the family that owned the castle.

181 bottom Only the conical roofs of the towers appear above the walls, giving the building a severe and heavy appearance.

Grandson

The victors took all the coins from Charles' treasury. In his desperate escape, the duke also lost a diamond "worth more than a province, one of the largest in Christianity." After changing hands many times, the gem was set in the crown of the French king. That victory and those riches changed Switzerland's destiny forever. From that day on, the mountaineers abandoned their hard work in the fields to become mercenaries. (G.G.)

Viewed from the lake, the outline of the castle – unmistakable – looks tapered, sleek, and elegant, with slender and delicate towers. In reality, the complex is quite varied. The quarters of the *Petit* and *Grand Château* are enclosed by a tall rectangular curtain wall that is nearly 200 feet long and slightly rounded toward the south, with three massive round towers and two semicircular ones. What remains of the old fortress of the Grandson family, whose crest bore a bell with the eloquent motto "*à petite cloche grand son*," is the outcome of centuries of remodeling. This is evident from the materials alone: tufa, Hauterive stone, and brick (the latter technique was imported from Piedmont). The most significant work was done in 1875, when Baron de Blonay purchased the castle and undertook extensive restoration work. In 1910, architect Otto Schmid renovated the east wing, and the restored feudal residence was equipped with all the latest 20th-century inventions. Following World War II, architect von Cabota recreated Renaissance rooms, the chapel, and the dungeons. An automobile museum was also opened. In 1983, it was purchased by the Zurich Foundation for art, culture, and history, and an exhibition on ancient weapons was inaugurated, including a section on the Burgundian wars. (G.R.)

182 bottom One of the rooms in the private apartments, which have been converted into a museum, is decorated with 18th-century furniture, Flemish tapestries, and hunting trophies.

183 bottom The grand fireplace dominates the dining room, furnished with "medieval" furniture made in the 19th century.

182-183 Beautiful 15th-century armor is displayed in the Knights' Hall. This armor is similar to the kind worn by the Burgundian noblemen routed by the Swiss mountaineers in the Battle of Grandson in 1476.

Gruyères
SWITZERLAND

184 top Two homini salvatici *hold the coat of arms with the crane, the emblem of the Counts of Gruyères, in this colorful stained-glass window from the 16th century.*

184 bottom The internal esplanade, which is higher than the walls around it, was transformed into a 16th-century-style Italian garden.

There were once countless *gruyères* in French-speaking countries. In fact, the term *gruyère* or *gruerie* meant a wooded and marshy area where cranes would stop twice a year when they migrated from Scandinavia to Africa and back. During the Middle Ages, when hunting was a popular pastime among nobles, the cranes were guarded by a *grand gruyer*, who answered directly to the king. However, the most famous *gruyère* in the world is in the Swiss canton of Fribourg. This area is famous not only for its exquisite cheese, but also for the deeds of its counts, who built a castle there that is essentially still intact. The castle was built in the 13th century. By this time, the Gruyères – initially subjects of the Holy Roman Empire and then Savoy vassals – had been a well-known and powerful family for at least 200 years. Most of the castle was remodeled in the 16th century. As soon as the renovation and decorative work was completed, however, the dynasty of the counts of Gruyères tragically declined. Raised by the court of King Francis I of France and then by the imperial court of Charles V, Michel, the last Count of Gruyères, inherited the family debts in 1538.

184-185 The castle rises on a hill over the village, which has essentially maintained its medieval appearance. Old houses line the main road, including the home of the counts' court jester.

185 bottom Despite the fact that much of the castle was remodeled during the 16th century, Gruyères has maintained the original layout of the medieval fortress, with its inaccessible round tower.

Gruyères

186 top The ever-present Gruyères crane and elegant garlands adorn the panels of the coffered ceiling in the Knights' Hall. The most fascinating room in the castle, it was decorated in the mid-19th century by the Genevan painter Bovy, following the neo-Gothic style in vogue during that period.

186 bottom left Bovy's panels narrate the episodes in Swiss history involving the Counts of Gruyères. This one depicts Count Rudolph III as he captures Hue Castle.

186 bottom right Wielding a heavy broadsword with both hands, Count Pierre IV routs the Bernese troops: this is another chapter in the saga of the Gruyères, depicted by Bovy in the Knights' Hall.

186-187 The Knights' Hall was completed in the mid-19th century. Illuminated by a large window, it features a coffered ceiling and large painted panels, and is furnished with Gothic-style pieces.

187 bottom Two members of the Gruyères family, following the squire holding the standard of the noble house, leave for the crusades. As the group of damsels bids them farewell, one of the women faints near the horses. This painting by Bovy is in the Knights' Hall.

These staggering debts had been amassed by his predecessors over years and years of extravagant spending. For over 15 years, Count Michel struggled to stay afloat, but in 1554, he finally attempted to solve his indebtedness by convening his vassals and begging them to help him balance his budget. In exchange, he pledged to abolish all his feudal rights. His subjects agreed, but for some reason the count fled that very evening, never to return to Gruyères. His property was split up between the cities of Bern and Fribourg, which settled his creditors' claims.

Fribourg installed its bailiffs here, and in the 19th century part, of the castle was converted into a prison, whereas the remainder housed the prefect's office. It was restored in several stages, starting in 1848. (G.G.)

188 top The Renaissance furnishings in the Hall of the Counts include Flemish tapestries with episodes from the life of Samson, a canopy bed, and a large fireplace.

188 bottom When the Bovy family restored the castle during the 19th century, painters like Jean-Baptiste-Camille Corot and Barthélemy Menn were commissioned to execute enchanting landscapes.

The original fortress was built near the tip of a rocky spur, but it was nothing more than an enormous keep with 13-foot-thick walls. A round tower was built in the southeast corner in 1270. The outside walls were raised in the 14th century, and a gatehouse and two shell-shaped towers were built to ensure lateral defense; there was also a chapel in one of the towers. In the 15th century, it was adapted to meet defensive needs. A *chemin de ronde* was created along the crest, linking the different towers – including the Square Tower and the Savoyard Tower – and extending to the town below it. In about 1490, the stronghold was renovated in Renaissance style. The Bovy family purchased it in 1848, saving it from demolition. Its new owners were art lovers (Daniel Bovy studied with Ingres) and they restored the castle to its former splendor. In fact, it is now the most visited castle in Switzerland, second only to Chillon. It boasts an exquisite chapel built in 1480, which features the ribbing typical of the flamboyant Gothic style, and the Burgundy Hall, which has relics from the Battle of Morat (1476), three extremely rare and priceless ceremonial mantles of the Order of the Golden Fleece. The Bovy family also decorated the Knights' Hall with paintings of the *Deeds and Legends of the Counts of Gruyères* and furnished many of the rooms with important pieces. The Count's Chamber has four Flemish tapestries, the walls in the Bailiffs' Hall are decorated with Baroque works, and there are four landscapes by Corot in the Main Hall. (G.R.)

188-189 For more than two centuries, the castle was the home of the Fribourg bailiffs, whose influence is evident in the Bailiffs' Hall, furnished in the Baroque style.

189 bottom The end of the 15th century marks a glorious phase in the history of the counts of Gruyères. After fighting as the Confederates' ally in the Swiss-Burgundian War, Count Louis decided to modernize the castle. The chapel was also built during this period. The castle was turned into an aristocratic residence, losing its original fortress-like appearance.

Gruyères

Fénis

ITALY

As visitors descend from Aosta toward the Piedmont region along the Dora Valley, a dark, intricate-looking structure comes into sight. Upon approach, it reveals a picturesque labyrinthine tangle of curtain walls, towers, *bartizans*, crenellated *chemins de ronde* and corner towers set on a small plateau overlooking the valley floor. This is the castle of Fénis, one of the many owned by the Challant family, which wielded enormous power in the county of Aosta. Aimone di Challant, a leading figure at the court of Savoy, started building it in about 1340, and his son Bonifacio completed it toward the end of the century. It thus became the regular residence of the family, which resided there until the early 1700s. Alfredo D'Andrade, a medievalist architect, purchased it in 1895. He did extensive restoration work on the castle and then transferred it to the Italian government. More scientific restoration was done on it in 1935-36.

The exterior of Fénis evokes the feudal system of the Middle Ages, with knights and damsels, jesters and minstrels. However, the interior, with beautiful living quarters, is an outstanding example of the 15th-century transition of these structures from fortress to noble residence. This patina of courtly civilization overlaying powerful military architecture is most evident in the chapel and courtyard frescoes by Giacomo Jaquerio and his workshop, reflecting the elegant lines of the international Gothic. (G.G.)

190 top The castle's current appearance is the outcome of restoration done at the turn of the 20th century and then in the 1930s, in order to eliminate alterations done after the 15th century and recreate its medieval appearance.

190 bottom The rustic round tower, compact and virtually devoid of openings, rises above the merlons of the outside wall overlooking the town.

190-191 A double row of walls surrounds the vibrant central portion, which has a complex pentagonal plan flanked by towers of different sizes as well as projecting towers.

191 bottom *The large square tower in the middle was the original construction, and the lords of Challant subsequently added increasingly large buildings around it.*

An ancient tower may have guarded a pyrite mine here during the Roman era. The castle developed around the tower and was part of the Savoyard rulers' defensive system. What remains of the early structure is the square tower, which was the central part of the castle. Fénis, located on a grassy knoll overlooking the village, has three sets of fortified walls and numerous towers that rise from a pentagonal ground plan. At the end of the square internal courtyard, a massive yet elegant semicircular staircase, with a fresco of Saint George, leads to a double gallery with a loggia, decorated with frescoes done in the first half of the 15th century and attributed to Giacomo Jaquerio. The chapel inside the castle is magnificent, with frescoes by Jaquerio (1425-30) of *The Crucifixion*, *Our Lady of Mercy*, *Saint John the Baptist*, and *Michael the Archangel*. Following the restoration work of 1936, the complex was converted into the Val d'Aosta Furniture Museum, with furnishings and objects from the 15th to the 17th century. (G.R.)

Fénis

192 bottom Fully outfitted in armor and wearing an elegant cloak, Saint Michael the Archangel crushes Satan in this fresco done by Giacomo Jaquerio in the castle chapel between 1425 and 1430.

193 top A throng of somber commoners brings offerings and petitions to two benedictory bishops, Uberto and Grato, in one of the anonymous 15th-century frescoes decorating the walls of the courtyard.

193 bottom The frescoes in the chapel are among the masterpieces of Giacomo Jaquerio. Unfortunately, there are very few extant works by this artist. His Crucifixion is shown in this picture.

192-193 In the internal courtyard, there is a semicircular staircase with a fresco of Saint George killing the dragon and freeing a princess. The stairs lead to an elegant loggia decorated with a cycle of paintings attributed to Giacomo Jaquerio, a 15th-century Piedmontese painter.

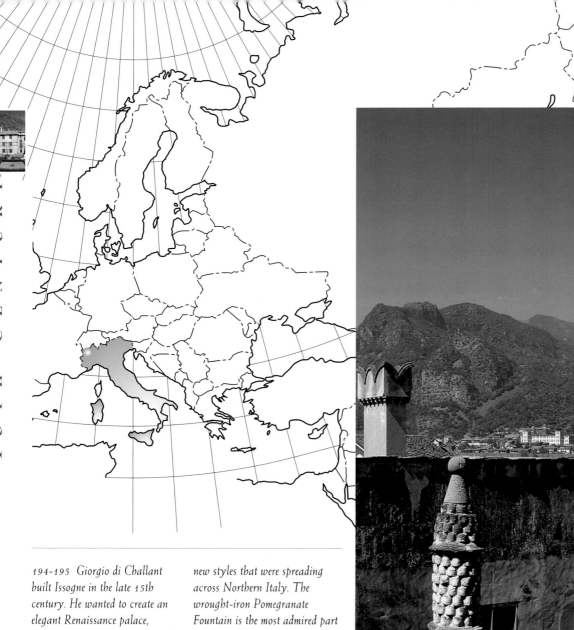

194-195 Giorgio di Challant built Issogne in the late 15th century. He wanted to create an elegant Renaissance palace, decorating and furnishing it in the new styles that were spreading across Northern Italy. The wrought-iron Pomegranate Fountain is the most admired part of the castle.

Challant

ITALY

Verrès, a small town in the Dora Valley that has maintained its neat medieval appearance, is dominated by the massive yet compact structure of a stronghold considered one of the most typical examples of Aosta's military architecture. The nearby Castle of Issogne is by contrast the model of a noble residence combining Gothic and Renaissance elements. Both Verrès and Issogne belonged to the Challant family. The former was built between 1360 and 1390, though the curtain wall was built in the 1500s. The latter was constructed by Giorgio di Challant, a clergyman, humanist, and restless spirit who had traveled extensively across Europe. He began building the castle in 1480, furnishing it so lavishly that it was considered "the most noble palace in the States of Savoy." At the end of the 19th century, Issogne was purchased by Vittorio Avondo, who restored it, bringing in a collection of furniture and artwork

to recreate a 15th-century atmosphere. In 1907 Avondo donated the castle to the Italian government, which completed the restoration work in 1935-36.

The castle's horizontal construction and the layout of its masonry structures reflect Renaissance concepts, but its decoration is late Gothic, particularly the lovely courtyard with vivid frescoes of the coats of arms and valiant deeds of the most illustrious representatives of the Challant family. The objective of these works was to edify the later generations, and according to the faded inscription on the wall, *le miroir pour les enfants de Challant*, they were meant to be "a mirror for the Challant children." The frescoes in the lunettes of the portico are famous. The work of an anonymous painter, they portray scenes from everyday life: the bakery, the tailor's shop, the butcher's shop, the market, and the guard corps. (G.G.)

195 bottom On the first floor, an airy loggia overlooks the courtyard, whose arches are supported by thick Nordic-style pillars. The internal façade is decorated with lovely frescoes depicting the deeds of the Challant family.

Seen from the outside, the castle is an enormous building without any distinctive features except for its tower-shaped chimneystacks. The interior is set around a small courtyard that is the only example of a garden in a Val d'Aosta castle. The nearby tower was set up for falconry. The castle harmoniously merges two styles: the Italian Renaissance and the Northern Renaissance (with low arches, loggias, and windows reflecting a Burgundian influence). The splendid, wrought-iron Pomegranate Fountain (which was originally brightly painted), the work of blacksmiths Pantaleone de Lalaz and Nicolas Longbvet, dominates the middle of the courtyard. The spectacular rooms at Val d'Aosta's best-preserved castle hold unexpected medieval art treasures: frescoes, wooden panels, furniture, curious graffiti inscriptions on the walls of the corridors, a chapel with a wooden altar (a Burgundian masterpiece) and the famous Chamber of the King of France, which has an exquisite coffered ceiling decorated with gilded lilies against a pale blue background. (G.R.).)

197 top The chamber of Giorgio di Challant - whose coat of arms, borne by a griffin and a lion, is visible on the fireplace - is decorated with 16th-century frescoes and furnished with faux-Gothic pieces.

197 bottom The Chamber of the King of France was given this name because a French monarch used it during one of the numerous invasions of Italy. For his stay, the coffered ceiling was decorated with gold fleurs-de-lis against a pale blue background, the emblem of the French monarchy.

Challant

196-197 As the apothecary prepares a recipe, his servant weighs the ingredients for a damsel who has come to buy medicine at this 15th-century pharmacy, which looks very well-stocked.

196 bottom The cycle of frescoes painted under the portico of the internal courtyard portrays scenes from everyday life at the castle toward the end of the 15th century. This is one of the most vibrant and intriguing works remaining here.

Castello del Buon Consiglio
ITALY

During the Middle Ages, due to its strategic position in the Adige River valley the city of Trent controlled the most important road linking the two parts of the Holy Roman Empire: Italy and Germany. To ensure that this gateway would be in friendly hands, Emperor Conrad II (1024-39) created the ecclesiastical principality of Trent in 1027 and entrusted it to a bishop. At the time, these prelates, who had been granted secular powers, lived in a fortified building known as the Castelletto, located near the cathedral. In the mid-13th century, however, they decided that they needed a grander and more defensible residence.

As a result, they built the Castelvecchio, which is the oldest part of the Castello del Buon Consiglio. This allowed them to contend with the revolts of the local population against their often harsh use of power, while also defending the city against the attempts made by the counts of Tyrol to take over this territory. In 1407, however, the fortress was unable to hold out against the violence of the local population, which occupied the castle and imprisoned its despotic bishop, George of Liechtenstein (1440-93), in the Torre Vanga on the Adige River. His successors evidently learned their lesson, as they were much kinder toward their subjects.

199 top The imposing Great Tower, also known as the August Tower because it has traditionally - though wrongly - been attributed to the Roman era, rises above the battlements of the edifice below.

199 center The courtyard of Castelvecchio is lined with loggias on the different floors, creating a very picturesque effect. The fresco on the wall across from it, portraying Charlemagne and the bishops of Trent, was done by Fogolino in the early 16th century.

199 bottom The space between the buildings and the bastioned walls is occupied by an extensive garden that has been restored to recreate its late-18th-century appearance.

198-199 The imposing structure of the castle abuts the old city walls, which incorporated some of the castle towers. However, the castle also has its own set of walls - with round bastions - extending toward town.

Castello del Buon Consiglio

200 top In the Renaissance wing of Palazzo Magno, Girolamo Romani, better known as Romanino, frescoed the large five-arched loggia. The fresco on the vault depicts Phaeton's chariot.

200 bottom The frescoes in the lunette of the loggia portray elegantly garbed noblemen and ladies playing different musical instruments.

200-201 The loggia, which overlooks the Courtyard of the Lions, is decorated with four plaster medallions portraying four of the Hapsburg rulers: Maximilian I, Philip the Fair, Charles V, and Ferdinand I.

201 bottom left These four charming flautists, portrayed by Romanino on one of the lunettes, appear to be engrossed in their music.

201 bottom right In addition to courtly figures, Romanino's frescoes in the loggia also depict mythological, biblical, and historical Roman figures.

Castello del Buon Consiglio

In 1475, Johannes IV Hinderbach had the Castelvecchio modified, adding floors in the Venetian-Gothic style. However, it was the great Prince-Bishop Bernard of Cles who transformed the castle into an ornate Renaissance residence. He built Palazzo Magno (Great Palace) between 1528 and 1536 and called in famous Italian artists, who turned it into an extremely elegant and extraordinarily rich palace. The rule of his successor, Cristoforo Madruzzo, marked the golden age of the castle, when the city hosted the ecumenical council convened to draft the Catholic Church's response to the Protestant Reformation. The Council of Trent met intermittently from 1545 to 1562. Three other Madruzzo bishops ruled the principality until 1658. Claudia Particella, the mistress of Carlo Emanuele, the last of these bishops, was also the subject of a novel written by a young Benito Mussolini. The Giunta Albertina, a new structure connecting the Castelvecchio to Palazzo Magno, was built in the 17th century.

The ecclesiastical principality came to an end in May 1796 when the last bishop fled from the advancing French army commanded by Napoleon. When Trent passed to Austria, the castle was converted into barracks. It was restored after 1918 and now houses the National Museum of Trentino and the Risorgimento Museum. (G.G.)

202 top The vault of the Camera da Basso in the main tower, with stuccowork by Mantovani and Marcello Foligno, frames four episodes of Roman history painted by Fogolino.

202 bottom Fogolino painted an array of allegorical figures and fantastic creatures drawn from Greek and Roman mythology in the gores and ovals set around the ceiling in the Camera da Basso.

203 top The wood-paneled Hall of Justice has a lovely frescoed ceiling. Gores decorated with stuccowork frame the lunettes, painted with landscapes.

203 bottom Gothic Castelvecchio, with battlemented walls, has a lovely Venetian-style loggia and a projecting structure decorated with the coats of arms of two prince-bishops.

Albrecht Dürer's painting of the castle reveals that it was actually a series of structures. The most noteworthy of them was and still is the Torre dell'Aquila, an ancient defensive tower at the gates of Trent, boasting frescoes commissioned by Bishop George of Liechtenstein (1390-1419), including the cycles of the *Twelve Months* and of *Working the Fields*. The curtain wall built by Bernard of Cles is across from the tower. The castle was accessed through the Porta dei Diamanti, or Gate of Diamonds, so called because of the large ashlar stones framing it. The gate is located next to one of the three short towers that overlooked Renaissance gardens once filled with ancient statues. Various architects worked on the Castello del Buon Consiglio, but their names – many of which remain unknown – have been overshadowed by those of the artists commissioned to decorate the rooms: painters Dosso Dossi, Romanino, and Fogolino, sculptor Alessio Longhi, and Volterra sculptor Zaccaria Zacchi, who did the terracottas. Despite its three orders of loggias and pictorial decorations, the castle looks stark, and construction of a third body, the Giunta Albertina, in 1686-88 gave it a stately appearance. The elegant Venetian-style loggia in the middle evokes Palazzo Giovanelli in Venice. The Castello del Buon Consiglio now houses a museum. (G.R.)

204 left The Eagle's Tower was decorated by Prince-Bishop George of Liechtenstein. The cycle of frescoes depicting the 12 months has been attributed to the Bohemian painter Wenceslas. In this one, dedicated to December, woodsmen cut lumber and carry it into the city.

204 right The upper section of the September fresco depicts farmers plowing the fields. In the lower part, noblemen and ladies on horseback set out on a hunt with their falcons.

204-205 In July (left) and August (right), the figures are scything hay and gathering the harvest. However, one man has also taken advantage of the lovely weather to court a young lady.

205 bottom left October is dedicated to harvesting and pressing grapes in large vats. The rocky landscape in the background is quite unusual.

Castello del Buon Consiglio

*205 bottom right May, the
month of love: a merry company
leaves the turreted city and heads
to the countryside to enjoy
lighthearted conversation and a
delicious lunch.*

Castel Beseno

ITALY

The bastioned and turreted complex of Beseno occupies an entire hilltop of four acres, making it the largest fortified complex in Trentino. It was built in the middle of the Lagarina Valley between Rovereto and Trent, at the point where the road to Vicenza branched off from the Adige River valley. It was positioned to control the intersection of this important thoroughfare. The castle was first documented in 1171 and belonged to the Castelbarco family, which, allied with Verona, dominated the valley. To construct it, the family may have used rubble from enemy castles destroyed in 1166 to block the passage of the imperial troops of Frederick Barbarossa.

A century later, the Castelbarco family split up into five branches, one of which owned Castel Beseno. However, their splintered territory was reunited by Guglielmo da Castelbarco, who was podestà of Verona and who – according to an enduring but unproven legend – hosted Dante at Lizzana, one of the many castles he owned. Following Guglielmo's death, however, the Castelbarco property was split up again, this time among eight branches. Eager to annex Trent, the Venetian Republic took advantage of this weakness, and in the early 1400s it occupied the Lagarina Valley and a number of castles, including Beseno. When the Venetians lost the castle in 1470, the Trapp took it over, but it gradually fell into ruin. (G.G.)

The impressive ruins of Trent's last imperial-episcopal fortress against Venice are characterized by a double set of walls, which surround the stronghold to form a large ellipse (its long axis measures 820 feet). Beseno represents a response to the invention of artillery, making it a prime example of the transition from castle to fortress, and from fortress to bastions: in short, it represents an all-Italian discovery. Thus, towers on the old Castelbarco castle were lopped off and its walls were lowered (since attackers would no longer scale the curtains but would wait for a breach to be opened). Likewise, its battlements were replaced with merlons and long, low rounded parapets. At the same time, gun loops were created for flanking fire. Beseno was a stately residence that reflected its owners' high social standing, and many of its rooms have noteworthy frescoes painted between the 15th and 17th centuries. (G.R.)

206 bottom The complex structure of the fortress is the result of subsequent additions and modifications introduced to adapt this important stronghold to the progress made in military technology following the invention of artillery.

206-207 Castel Beseno was the key to the Lagarina Valley, controlling the road between the Adige River and Vicenza, and it was the center of power of the Castelbarco family, the lords of the valley.

207 bottom The entrance reveals the castle's composite nature: discordant rustic buildings rise over a wide, deep arch.

Castel Thun

ITALY

Anaunia or Val di Non is considered one of the most
beautiful valleys in Trentino. The area is famous for its
apples, but the valley also boasts a large number of castles:
25. Nevertheless, these strongholds are merely the ones that
survived repeated destructive attacks, because time and
again the valley people rebelled against embezzlements by
the Prince-Bishop of Trent, the feudal lord of the local
lands, and by local noblemen. Following the uprisings of
1407 and 1477, and above all the Rustic War of 1525 (a
Lutheran-inspired peasant rebellion), many of these castles
were razed. In turn, the aristocratic families of the valley –

some of whom allied with the Bishop of Trent and others
with his rival, the Count of Tyrol – were often at war,
attacking each other's castles and destroying them to their
very foundations. The Thun or Tono family stood out
amidst this bellicose mountain nobility and managed to
survive these troubled times virtually unscathed, remaining
in power until the 18th century. Castel Thun dates back to
the 13th century, but it was remodeled as an aristocratic
residence in 1569. This vast complex of buildings, which
was restored in 1925, is set on an isolated summit
surrounded by four bastioned walls. (G.G.)

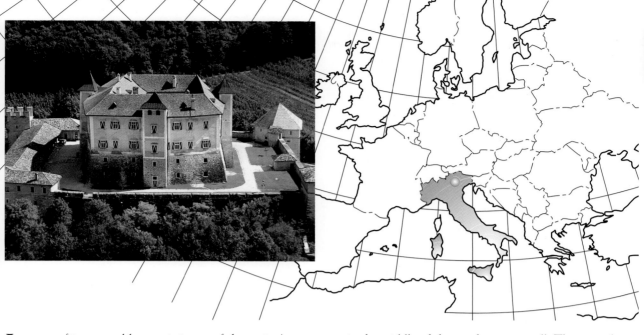

In terms of its general layout, it is one of the region's largest castles (150 rooms, one of which was used only for wakes). It belonged to the Thuns, a powerful family that ruled the Val di Non and Val di Sole. The family also owned the fortresses of Bragher, Caldes, and Castelfondo, and boasted that it owned the land from the Tonale Pass to Trent. Considered one of the most interesting examples of fortified architecture in Trentino, it is mainly Gothic in style. It is surrounded by a complex system of fortifications composed of towers, crescent-shaped bastions, a moat, a *chemin de ronde*, and an imposing gate referred to as the "Spanish Gate" (1566), made of massive ashlared stones and set in the middle of the north curtain wall. The central fortifications had a quadrangular ground plan, with sturdy ramparts and four towers. On the other side of the moat there was another wall with splayed embrasures and two battlemented towers built in the Middle Ages. Oddly, the towers were not built at the corners but in the middle of the façades. The loggia, which faces south (customary in mountain castles), gives the internal courtyard an elegant appearance. The castle was remodeled several times and finally transformed into a lavish country residence in 1668, when a member of the Thun family became the prince-bishop. (G.R.)

208-209 An enormous rectangular palace with a tower jutting from the façade is set in the middle of the fortified complex of Thun, one of the most impressive strongholds in Trentino.

209 top The palace, which was started in 1569, is a stunning example of Trent's noble residences during the Mannerist period, when the stylistic elements that had triumphed in Italy also reached this border region.

209 bottom Sigismondo Alfonso Thun, elected Prince-Bishop of Trent in 1668, embellished the castle and turned it into his favorite summer home, staying there for extended periods to escape the city heat.

Castel del Monte

ITALY

The compact, adamantine geometric structure of Castel del Monte, erected to dominate most of Puglia and Basilicata from one of the highest points on the Murge Plateau, is indubitably Italy's most striking example of 13th-century military architecture. Made of warm golden stone, the castle is one of the first – and purest – Gothic structures to rise in southern Italy. It was built by Emperor Frederick II (1215-50), the son of a Swabian father and a Norman-Sicilian mother. His extraordinary culture, mastery of languages including Arabic, keen intelligence and secular vision earned him the sobriquet *Stupor Mundi*, "Wonder of the World," and he was indeed a man ahead of his time. He was supposedly himself the architect of the castle, which was built between 1240 and 1250. However, Frederick did not construct it for military reasons alone. A passionate falconer (he even wrote a scholarly treatise about the subject in Latin), he decided to build his castle here because birds crossed the area during their annual migration. In addition to being a hunting lodge, this beautiful castle was also used for magnificent celebrations, such as the one in 1249 for the wedding of the emperor's illegitimate daughter Violante. In a fateful turn of events, after the fall of the Swabian dynasty the building was used to imprison Frederick's grandsons, the children of his son Manfred, who was killed during the Battle of Benevento.

Over the centuries that followed, the castle hosted the weddings of the Neapolitan royal family, but it was also used as a prison for enemies of the crown. Abandoned and left unguarded, the castle was later used by those fleeing the cities of Puglia during the plagues of the 17th century. Its marble work and sculptures were pillaged during the 18th century. Reduced to an empty stone shell, it was used by shepherds as shelter against bad weather, and as a base and hideout by bandits.

Castel del Monte was taken over by the Italian government in 1876 and completely restored. (G.G.)

210 top Frederick II of Swabia was a passionate falconer (he penned the treatise De arte venandi cum avibus on the subject) and he had Castel del Monte built on a plateau in Puglia that was along the route of migratory birds. The ruler is pictured here by a 19th-century artist.

210 bottom The castle has a perfectly octagonal layout accentuated by eight towers, which are also octagonal. It is divided into two stories, the upper one with double-lancet windows and the bottom with single-lancet ones.

210-211 The impressive geometric structure of Castel del Monte rises above the woods and countryside like a rocky island. The village seems to crouch along the slope to avoid disturbing the stronghold's solitary purity.

Castel del Monte

Hundreds – if not thousands – of studies on astronomic and astrological symbolism have examined this octagonal structure, which has eight octagonal towers at its corners, eight rooms on each of the two floors, and an octagonal courtyard. During the Middle Ages, geometry and magic were intertwined, and stargazers looked to the heavens for signs before any foundations could be laid. The octagonal complex in Puglia was an astronomical summa: this subtle interplay of balance and proportion reflected precise mathematical and geometric calculations. For example, the length of the shadow the inner brim of the roof casts in the courtyard was studied in relation to the season and the signs of the zodiac.

Castel del Monte is not an enormous castle, and its longest diagonal measures just 183 feet. The castle entrance, which faces east, was made of prized marble and closed by a pointed Gothic arch, and it is cited in all architectural manuals. The interior space is dominated by corner columns with Corinthian capitals. The towers feature the so-called "umbrella" vaults, or ribbed ceilings divided into six sections to resemble a canopy. The Gothic double-lancet windows with trilobate arches are quite small with respect to the enormous rooms. The castle has no defensive devices whatsoever: it is devoid of drawbridges, external curtains, moats, battlements, and murder holes. Nevertheless, the building was extremely modern for its era. It even had bathrooms and a complex plumbing system. The rooms were once finished with precious polychrome marble, mosaics, and paintings, but fragments of imperial crimson marble, visible on the windows and doors, are all that remain. (G.R.)

212-213 The unusual structure of the castle has spawned an array of esoteric interpretations. This is probably due also to the fame of a medieval scholar of the occult sciences, who accompanied his imperial builder and supposedly designed the castle himself.

213 top The rainwater drain in the middle of the courtyard was the linchpin of an elaborate and complex plumbing system that was well ahead of its time. It was probably built by the emperor's Sicilian-Arab workers, who were highly skilled in this art.

213 bottom Unfortunately, all the internal decorative work - polychrome marbles, mosaics, and frescoes - has disappeared, destroyed or pillaged over centuries of abandonment. The magnificent Gothic vaults - completely bare - are all that remain.

Miramare

ITALY

In 1854 Maximilian of Hapsburg, the younger brother of Emperor Franz Josef (1830-1916) was appointed commander-in-chief of the Austrian Navy. The 22-year-old blond admiral, enthralled by his new post, set about to fulfill it promptly and intelligently, moving to Trieste. He loved the empire's stately port city, and in 1856, he started building the castle of Miramare a few miles away. This white castle on the shores of the Adriatic was designed by architect Carlo Junker in a pseudo-medieval style that, at the time, was referred to as "Norman." Miramare became Maximilian's favorite residence, and he continued to live here with his wife Charlotte, the daughter of King Leopold of Belgium, even after he was appointed governor-general of the Lombardo-Veneto kingdom.

It was here that, in 1864, he welcomed a delegation of Mexican noblemen who offered him the imperial crown of their country, torn apart by civil war. The day before – in the very same room – he had formally relinquished his succession rights to the Hapsburg Empire and embraced his brother Franz Joseph for the last time. When Maximilian and Charlotte embarked from Miramare a few days later, the Mexican flag fluttered from castle's unfinished towers and a throng of Triestines bade them farewell.

Their anachronistic imperial adventure ended tragically in 1867. Captured by Mexican revolutionaries, Maximilian ended up in front of a firing squad. Charlotte, who had returned to Europe to seek military aid that no government could – or would – give her, lost her mind. In fact, Emperor Napoleon III,

who had convinced Maximilian to pursue his dream by promising his support, had already withdrawn the French troops. On the verge of madness, Charlotte returned to Miramare, where the increasingly worse news from Mexico finally drove her insane. She was never informed of her husband's death, and a few months later her father brought her back to Belgium, giving her the castle of Laeken as her residence. She lived here for half a century and died at the age of 86, never regaining her sanity. Every spring she would have a boat set up in the moat, go aboard, and announce, "We're leaving for Mexico!" Miramare, cloaked in an aura of tragic misfortune, remained deserted. After World War I and the fall of the Hapsburg Empire, it became the residence of the Duke of Aosta. It now houses a history museum. (G.G.)

214-215 Miramare is more like a country estate than a true castle. Built on a small promontory jutting into the Gulf of Trieste, it was the home of a dreamer who loved nature and the sea.

214 bottom and 215 top Statues, herms, vases, and columns dot the Italian garden that is part of the sprawling 55-acre park around the castle.

215 bottom Wedged gracefully between the sapphire sea and the luxuriant grounds, the white building was constructed by the architect Junker in a pseudo-medieval style referred to at the time as "Norman," though it had few medieval or Norman elements.

Miramare

White Istrian stone from the Orsera quarries, which had supplied Venice for 1,000 years, was used to build the castle. It has two floors and a mezzanine, with a battlemented tower overlooking the sea. As requested by Maximilian, its surroundings combined a lush natural setting with a view of the sea. The park around it covers nearly 55 acres. The interior decorations were designed by Franz and Julius Hofmann, woodworkers and gilders from Trieste. Following Maximilian's instructions, they created the oak ceilings and paneling in an old English style, even reproducing the aft wardroom of the S.M.S. *Novara*. The castle has more than 20 rooms, which still have their valuable original furnishings (including paintings by Caffi, Gürlitt, and Dell'Acqua). The Audience Hall, the ornate library, and the chapel, finished in Lebanese cedar supposedly given to Maximilian by Trieste's Greek community, are particularly striking. (G.R.)

216 top A portrait of the archduchess, set in a niche, is the highlight of Charlotte's chamber, named after Maximilian's unfortunate consort. This is where the she spent the last happy days of her life before the couple embarked on their tragic Mexican adventure.

216 bottom The master bedroom, decorated in an overblown style typical of the 19th century, has an enormous canopy bed and a dazzling Bohemian crystal chandelier.

216-217 Portraits of the members of Europe's royal families related to Maximilian and Charlotte hang in the Audience Hall, which was also the anteroom to the master bedroom (in the picture, the bed is visible through the door).

217 bottom Charlotte, on the dock at Miramare, welcomes her sister-in-law Elizabeth of Austria, the wife of Emperor Franz Joseph. The Emperor is stepping onto the stairs toward his brother Maximilian, who is bareheaded. The tender is flying the Union Jack because the boat belonged to a yacht lent to Elizabeth by Queen Victoria.

218-219 *The Hall of Justice, shown in this photograph, is one of Miramare's most sumptuous rooms. It is decorated in a vaguely Byzantine style.*

Miramare

219 bottom The library, full of beautiful leather-bound books, was a must in any aristocratic residence, but Maximilian happened to be an avid reader who was especially fond of historiography.

218 bottom In this hall, referred to as the Throne Room following Maximilian's coronation as the emperor of Mexico, the family tree illustrated with portraits proudly recreates the lineage of the House of Austria.

219 top The chapel, paneled in Lebanese cedar, reflects an odd and mismatched accumulation of styles. It was donated to Maximilian by Trieste's Greek community.

Castello Sforzesco

ITALY

220-221 Surrounded by the ellipse of 19th-century buildings that replaced the bastioned walls, the castle is separated from the dense urban sprawl by a small park, all that remains of the Sforzas' vast hunting reserve.

220 bottom During the 16th century, Milan's Spanish rulers updated the 15th-century complex to adapt it to new military requirements, building six bastions around it. In turn, the bastions were protected by a deep moat, as shown in this plan dated 1646.

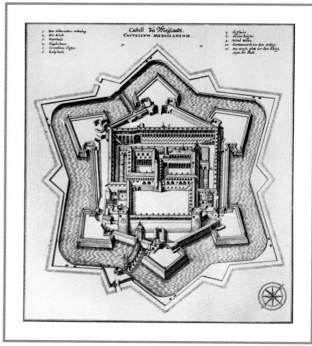

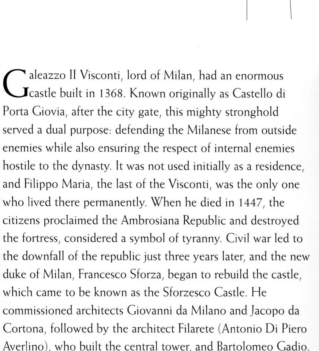

221 top Galeazzo Maria Sforza, Duke of Milan from 1466 to 1476 and shown here in a portrait attributed to Zanetto Bugatto, started the work to convert the castle into a lavish princely dwelling, adding the residential portions.

221 bottom The Visconti snake, adopted by the Sforzas, is quartered with the imperial eagle (Milan was a fiefdom of the Holy Roman Empire). The crest is set above the entry arch, with the initials of Duke Francesco Sforza.

Galeazzo II Visconti, lord of Milan, had an enormous castle built in 1368. Known originally as Castello di Porta Giovia, after the city gate, this mighty stronghold served a dual purpose: defending the Milanese from outside enemies while also ensuring the respect of internal enemies hostile to the dynasty. It was not used initially as a residence, and Filippo Maria, the last of the Visconti, was the only one who lived there permanently. When he died in 1447, the citizens proclaimed the Ambrosiana Republic and destroyed the fortress, considered a symbol of tyranny. Civil war led to the downfall of the republic just three years later, and the new duke of Milan, Francesco Sforza, began to rebuild the castle, which came to be known as the Sforzesco Castle. He commissioned architects Giovanni da Milano and Jacopo da Cortona, followed by the architect Filarete (Antonio Di Piero Averlino), who built the central tower, and Bartolomeo Gadio.

When the duke died in 1466, the main structures had already been completed, and his successor Galeazzo Maria had the residential parts added, including the Rocchetta. However, it was Ludovico il Moro who turned the Sforzesco Castle into the most magnificent noble residence in Italy. Not only did he commission the best artists in Lombardy to decorate it, but he also called in Bramante and Leonardo da Vinci. The banquets and festivities held at the castle astonished guests with their extravagance and splendor, particularly those celebrating the wedding of Gian Galeazzo Sforza and Isabella of Aragon in 1489, and Ludovico's own marriage to Beatrice d'Este two years later.

This magnificence was short-lived. When the French invaded Milan in 1499, Ludovico fled and the castle surrendered without a fight. Instead, it took Massimiliano Sforza nearly a year to win it back from the French in 1513. Just two years later, he had to defend it against them once again, but was quickly forced to surrender. The castle was seriously damaged in 1521 when it was struck by lightning and a powder magazine in one of the towers exploded. The

Castello Sforzesco

Spanish, Milan's new rulers, restored the castle and surrounded the 15th-century structure with ramparts and bastions, transforming it into a well-fortified citadel. These fortifications proved useless. The castle's successive conquerors – from the imperial army to the Savoy, the Spanish, the Austrian armies, and also Napoleon's forces and the Russians – managed to capture it with very little effort. Napoleon had the citadel destroyed but the castle was left intact.

During their post-Waterloo period of rule, the Austrians used the castle as an army barracks, and it was from here that Marshal Radetzky bombed the rebellious city during the Five Days of Milan in 1848. By 1880, the Sforzas' former marvel was in such poor shape that it was slated for demolition. However, the Lombard Historical Society managed to save it and radical restoration work, headed by architect Luca Beltrami, helped recreate part of the castle's original appearance. (G.G.)

222-223, 222 bottom right and 223 Amidst the polychrome crests of the Sforza dynasty, the statue of Saint Ambrose, patron saint of Milan, stands in a benedictory pose next to the Filarete Tower, facing the city center.

222 bottom left Two imposing round ashlared towers stand at the corners of the enormous quadrangular building.

What remains of one of Europe's largest strongholds is an enormous castle with a square ground plan. The Filarete Tower divides the long façade extending between two round ashlarwork towers, the Torrione di Santo Spirito and the Torrione dei Carmini, and was designed to conceal the castle's impregnable structure with a reassuringly elegant appearance. Inside the stronghold, the innermost refuge, the Rocchetta, and the rectangular Ducal Courtyard are located past the main courtyard, dominated by the Tower of Bona of Savoy and enclosed by square towers at the four corners. The castle houses extraordinary museums, with masterpieces such as Michelangelo's *Rondanini Pietà*, the twelve Trivulzio Tapestries of the *Months*, Bambaia's *Effigy of Gaston de Foix*, and paintings by Mantegna, Lotto, Luini, and Van Dyck. The Castle Art Museums also boast one of the world's finest collections of antique musical instruments, as well as collections of majolica, furniture and other artifacts. The famous Biblioteca Trivulziana library, the Bertarelli Print Collection, the Medal Collection, and the Milan Stamp Collection are also housed within the castle's terracotta walls. (G.R.)

Castello Sforzesco

224 *Filarete's Tower, in the middle of the façade, is crowned by a small battlemented tower and a majestic lantern, and it is the castle's most spectacular tower.*

225 top *The windows of the Rocchetta are decorated with terracotta cornices typical of the Lombard area. The Rocchetta was*

the section of the castle that housed the duke's private apartments, but it was also the last redoubt in the event of an attack.

225 bottom *Geometric decorations give the façades of the wings facing the courtyard an elegant appearance.*

Castel dell'Ovo

ITALY

226 bottom The flooring of this vaulted underground passage is actually the bedrock of the ancient island, which is now connected to the mainland.

226-227 The compact block of constructions that have accumulated over the centuries takes up the entire island across from Santa Lucia, the port celebrated by Neapolitan songs.

Castel Dell'Ovo, built on a small rocky island connected to the mainland by a short causeway, is located in one of the most charming parts of Naples. The massive castle overlooks the port of Santa Lucia, and its yellow curtain walls, reflected in the gulf, paint a striking picture. This islet was the site of a building that was part of the magnificent villa owned by the wealthy Roman patrician Lucullus. After the fall of the Roman Empire, a group of Basilian monks built a monastery over the ruins. The Normans exploited this strategic position to build a fortress, which Frederick II (1215-50) enlarged and fortified with towers to safeguard the imperial treasury.

After the death of Frederick's successor, Emperor Conrad IV (1250-54), Charles of Anjou seized Naples and imprisoned Conradin, Conrad's son and heir, before beheading him in 1268. He also held Princess Beatrice, daughter of Conrad IV's illegitimate half-brother Manfred, captive in Castello d'Ovo but she was liberated in 1284 when Sicilian-Aragonese admiral Roger of Loria raided the castle.

The name "Castel dell'Ovo" was first used in the 12th century, supposedly because of the structure's ovoid, or egglike layout. According to local legends, however, Virgil – who during the Middle Ages was acknowledged not only as a great poet but also a powerful magus – had an iron cage hung in one of the rooms of the castle. An amphora inside it held an enchanted egg, and it was said that if the egg broke, the castle was doomed. Indeed, disaster struck during the reign of Queen Joan I (1343–82) who had the castle rebuilt by creating another egg to replace the original one. Joan was held prisoner in her own castle during the dynastic wars that raged in her kingdom.

The castle was not used as a residence until the era of the first Angevin rulers (1266-1382), but after this period it was again used exclusively for military purposes as the city's maritime defense. It was besieged and bombarded a number of times, conquered in 1420 by the Aragonese, in 1495 by the French, and in 1503 by the Spanish, who demolished much of the castle when they exploded a mine. It was rebuilt, and a round seagirt redoubt was added in 1691 by architect Ferdinando de Grunenberg, who gave the castle its current form. It was attacked in 1733, when Charles of Bourbon bombarded it before his victorious entrance to Naples, and again in 1799, when the patriots of the Parthenopean Republic took refuge here to escape the Sanfedists. In the 19th century, it was transformed into barracks. (G.G.)

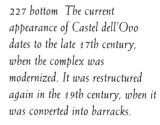

227 bottom The current appearance of Castel dell'Ovo dates to the late 17th century, when the complex was modernized. It was restructured again in the 19th century, when it was converted into barracks.

The structure of Castel dell'Ovo is as intriguing as it is complex: it is the outcome of hundreds of years of destruction and reconstruction, overlays and restoration. This elongated complex extends from the seafront (according to local legend, its name stems from its elliptical layout).

A large arch connects the two parts of the islet of Megaris, and tall walls on the landward side enclose medieval buildings, 16th- and 17th-century towers, Angevin and Aragonese loggias, barracks, and casemates aligned along an internal road. Restoration work conducted over the past 40 years has recreated the stately appearance of its rooms, including the Hall of Columns and the Church of the Savior. The castle, which is owned by the Italian Ministry of Culture, is now used as an exhibition and convention venue. (G.R.)

Predjama

SLOVENIA

On the Karst Plateau, just a few miles from the magical cavern of Postojna (the second largest in the world), an entire castle was built inside another enormous cave carved out of the side of a dramatic 400-foot cliff.

The locals referred to this immense opening as *Lunkja*, the Hole. A castle was built here in the 1300s and it was taken over by the Lueger family at the end of the century. In 1478, Erazem Lueger inherited the fiefdom and the fortress, but instead of remaining faithful to the Hapsburg emperor Frederick III (1440-93), he allied himself with the Hungarian king Matthias

Corvinus (1458-1490). Frederick reacted by murdering Erazem's best friend, the knight Andreas Baumkirchner, and Erazem avenged his death by killing one of the emperor's relatives. Arrested and imprisoned, he managed to escape and return to his fief, an impenetrable wooded territory, taking refuge in the safe and virtually invisible castle concealed in the cave. Using the castle as their base, he and his followers began to attack and loot caravans bringing goods from the port of Trieste to the inland areas. The sovereign ordered the governor of Trieste to stop the robberies, but finding Erazem was far from simple. The

228-229 Nothing remains of the first castle, which was built by the Lueger family in the 14th century but fell into ruin. A more elegant Renaissance building was built over the original structure, maintaining its layout.

229 top The crest of the Cobenzl family, quartered with the imperial eagle, is painted between the windows of the side facing town.

229 bottom Predjama means "in front of the cave," and no name could be more appropriate for this castle. Part of it is set in a rocky hollow that is over 5,500 feet long and nearly 400 feet high.

governor searched long and hard, and he finally discovered the Slovenian Robin Hood's hideout by following footprints and tracks in the snow. The castle perched on the mountainside was assaulted and its attackers were convinced those inside would soon surrender out of hunger.

However, Erazem smuggled supplies into the castle through a tunnel in the mountain leading to the forest, and he mocked his besiegers by launching catapults full of food. Betrayal ultimately led to the rebel's downfall. In exchange for a large sum of money, one of Erazem's servants told the governor that

every evening his master went to a point in the castle directly over the cliff. This is where the latrines were located, and the elusive castellan naturally had to go there in person. The traitor marked the spot with a white cloth, the governor's gunners aimed and, upon the servant's signal, they fired, burying Erazem under the rocks shattered by the cannonades.

The castle went to the Luegers' female descendants and then to the Cobenzl family, but it was in such poor condition that it was abandoned. In 1570, it was replaced with a new castle built outside the cave in the elegant Renaissance style visible today. (G.G.)

230-231 Gripping a broadsword like a true warrior, an ancestor of the Cobenzl family stares at visitors from a portrait hanging in one of the halls on the upper floor.

Predjama

This toponym means "in front of the cave," because the castle is set at the entrance to an enormous cavern. The most surprising thing about it is the way the building was adapted to fit into these natural surroundings. The earliest documentation of the original stronghold, referred to as Jama, goes back to the 14th century, but the building we see today was built in the 16th century. In 1567, the Cobenzl family built a new castle on a platform carved from bare rock outside the cave, although part of the structure is set under the sheer face of the cliff. An entrance was built in a tower connected to the road by a wooden bridge. The entrance to the previous castle, which was once entered via a drawbridge, is across from it.

The edifice rises from east to west and reaches its maximum height right in the cave. As opposed to the other structures, the corners of the entrance tower are made of limestone blocks overlapped to form "anchored" corners. The date 1570, the year the central part was completed, is visible over the Cobenzl coat of arms. There were only a few rooms in the castle, due to the fact that the rockface behind it limited the depth of the structure. Many of the stairs leading to the upper floors are set against bare rock. Naturally, there is a chapel, located between the central area and the east wing. Dedicated to Saint Anne, it was richly furnished. A long, famous secret passage – now closed off by an iron gate – leads to the woods on the plateau, and it was used to bring supplies to the castle, circumventing attackers. (G.R.)

231 Another mannequin waits to be served his dinner in this hall, which is decorated with 19th-century furniture replicating the Gothic style.

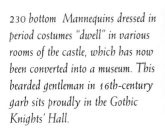

230 bottom Mannequins dressed in period costumes "dwell" in various rooms of the castle, which has now been converted into a museum. This bearded gentleman in 16th-century garb sits proudly in the Gothic Knights' Hall.

232 *Two large wings with loggias, designed by an Italian architect, were added to the square keep, or Red Tower, during the Renaissance.*

Sárospatak
HUNGARY

Sárospatak Castle, built in the 13th century, is located in the northern part of the Tokaji winemaking region, along the banks of the Bodrog River near the modern-day Slovakian border. The Hungarian magnate Peter Perényi had it completely rebuilt as a luxurious Renaissance residence, commissioning Italian architect Alessandro da Vedano to oversee the project. The work began in 1534, and following Peter's death it was completed by his son Gábor. When Gábor died in 1567 without leaving any direct heirs, the castle went to György Rákóczi, who turned it into a small but splendid court in 1616. Rákóczi embellished the castle and continued to live there even after he was elected voivode of Transylvania in 1630. The principality was formally a vassal of the Ottoman Empire, and Rákóczi attempted to maintain its independence by maintaining the middle ground between the Austrians and the Turks. Ferenc II Rákóczi, born in 1676, maintained this policy against Austria, which at the end of the 17th century seized Hungary and Transylvania, defeating the Turks. He sought the support of the Sun King, and from 1703 to 1711 he headed an anti-Austrian revolt referred to as the Kuruc rising, or "the Crusaders."

During this period, many of Austria's enemies acknowledged him as prince regent of Hungary, and Sárospatak Castle received numerous foreign ambassadors who were accredited with his court. When the Austrians finally managed to crush the uprising, Rákóczi was forced to abandon the castle, going into exile. He moved to France and lived at Versailles with his most loyal fighters, who refused to leave him. His men joined the forces of Louis XIV and became light-cavalry instructors: the famous Hussars. Abandoned for many years, Sárospatak Castle virtually fell into ruin. In the 19th century, it was purchased by the Bretzenheim and then by the Windischgratz family, and was saved through sweeping restoration work. (G.G.)

The castle overlooking what is known as "the Hungarian Cambridge" and "the Athens of the Bodrog" combines great fortified architecture with the features of Hungarian residences: cusped round towers, thick walls, loggias, and courtyards with Serlian windows. Construction began in 1534, and the oldest portion is the impressive structure known as the *Red Tower*, which boasts the stylistic elements of the Gothic and late-Renaissance periods. The upper floors of the west, north, and south wings were built under György Rákóczi, Prince of Transylvania. The arched loggia connecting the tower to the west wing and the staircase were built in 1646, and the secret balcony dates to 1651. The castle fell into ruin toward the end of the 17th century. It has since been restored, and the late-Renaissance Lorantffy loggia, the Prince's Palace, and the library are splendid. The old church was built in the 14th century and it is one of the most magnificent examples of Hungarian Gothic. Its walls are decorated with paintings by Franz Anton Maulbertsch, and its Baroque organ and wooden altar are famous. Today, there is a collection of memorabilia connected with the history of the Rákóczis as well as artifacts about winemaking and the production of porcelain. In the 19th century, the Bretzenheims built the Romanesque frontal and installed the English park. The Windischgratz family later had the Chapel of St. Elizabeth built in the *Red Tower*. (G.R.)

233 top *The round Sub Rosa Room was named after the beautiful stone rose in the keystone. It is the most striking room in the castle.*

233 bottom *The elegant forms of the staircase and the arched loggia date to the mid-17th century, when the castle had already been taken over by the Rákóczi princes of Transylvania and was converted into a small but splendid court.*

Gondar Castle

ETHIOPIA

As in medieval Europe, the heavenly powers loved to interfere with earthly affairs in the Christian kingdom of Ethiopia, which according to a poetic legend was founded by the descendants of Solomon and the Queen of Sheba. At the beginning of the 16th century, while the country was tormented by the Muslim invasions, an angel appeared in a dream to the monarch Lebna Dengel, ordering him to establish his capital in a place whose name began with the letter G. Until then, the Negus Neghesti – the "King of Kings" – did not have a stable residence; his was a transhumant court that moved from one end of this vast empire to the other, depending on military requirements or the need for food. It took a whole century to find the place indicated by the heavens, for the winged messenger had been too enigmatic. Guzara, on the banks of Lake Tana, was chosen at first, and then in about 1610 King Susenyos moved further north, to Gorgora.

However, it was King Susenyo's son Fasilidas who ultimately identified the fateful "G" as Gondar, which was a fairly insignificant village in the hilly, fertile province of Dembea. In 1635, he built a large complex of fortified buildings here, and a city developed around it. To decorate his new palace, which

235 *The castle of Iyasu I, a contemporary of the Sun King, was probably designed by Yemenite architects. The wide battlements with rounded merlons are typically Arabian in style.*

234-235 *This picture was taken from the top of Fasilidas' castle. The structure overlooks the vast complex of the ruins of Gondar, whose palace comprised a series of separate buildings. Each one was used for a specific function or assigned to a member of the numerous royal family.*

234 bottom *Fasilidas' castle is composed of a battlemented central rectangular structure with 4 round towers at the corners. Of the buildings that made the ancient Ethiopian capital a 17th-century marvel, the castle is the best preserved.*

seems to have been built by Yemenite and Hindu workers, Fasilidas turned to the rulers of the two most sumptuous empires of the era, sending his ambassadors to the Sultan of Constantinople and the Great Mogul of Agra. Nevertheless, what remains of his buildings has a Hindu-Portuguese appearance. During the preceding century, in fact, Portuguese soldiers and Jesuits were highly influential in Ethiopia, ultimately converting Susenyos to Catholicism. However, his subjects rebelled and forced him to abdicate. After driving out the Jesuits, Fasilidas reestablished the Coptic Church and dotted his new capital with religious buildings, monasteries and churches, which he devoutly financed. The Abuna, the Coptic patriarch, was granted an entire district in Gondar, which grew in both size and wealth under the founder's successors: Yohannes I (who added a library and chancery to the imperial palace) and, above all, Iyasu I. The latter ruled from 1682 to 1706 and transformed the city into the most important trading center in the Horn of Africa, attracting travelers from Europe, the Near East, Arabia, India, and Persia.

Louis XIV sent the physician Poncet as a court ambassador, and Poncet returned to Paris with such an astonishing report of the marvels of Gondar that no one believed him. Iyasu had a new castle – or rather, a new palace – constructed next to the one built by Fasilidas. According to popular accounts, both were the settings for orgies that almost always culminated with the hapless participants falling into evil traps.

The splendid Gondar of the 17th century gradually declined during the following century. Its commercially advantageous position was not central enough to allow the Negus to control the large fiefs of the faraway provinces, and legal authority slowly disintegrated. Finally, after conquering, sacking, and setting fire to the city, in 1855, King Tewodros moved the capital to Debra Tabor, and Gondar's castles and churches fell into ruin. (G.G.)

Fasilidas' castle, made of basalt, is laid out on two floors, with square and round towers at its corners. The castle rises amidst a large group of ruins that include remains of the royal palaces, encircled by thick defensive walls. The palace of Iyasu II can also be seen amidst the ruins. Built by Christian masons, it once had lavishly decorated rooms – now gone – that boasted Venetian mirrors and sumptuous objects worthy of the finest European palaces. The castle architecture of Gondar clearly reflects the influence of faraway Europe, particularly in its crenellated walls. However, its circular domed towers and arched windows are typically Arabian in appearance. (G.R.)

The Red Fort, Delhi

INDIA

The Mogul empire was at its apex in 1635 when Shah Jahan of Agra, whose name means "King of the world," ordered the construction of a new capital next to old Delhi: Shahjahanabad. In 1638, he moved into what was still a dusty and noisy building yard, and the following year, after his astrologers had carefully calculated the most favorable day, he laid the first stone of his new palace, known as Lal Qila or the Red Fort. It took nine years to complete this magnificent building, which is over half a mile long and nearly 2,000 feet wide, at a cost of nearly 130 tons of silver to pay for the work. The city walls, the gardens, and the Jami Masjid mosque, which could accommodate 40,000 people, cost 55 tons of silver.

The palace, circled by battlemented red sandstone walls and by the waters of the Jumna River, housed 10,000 Imperial Guards as well as countless other servants. There were thousands of horses in its stables, and its kitchens could feed the entire city. There were court tailors and jewelers, musicians whose performances indicated where the emperor was and what he was doing at that very moment, harem eunuchs and courtesans, jugglers who performed on the backs of elephants, and ministers who governed a state larger than all of Europe. Twice a day, when Shah Jahan stepped out on

236-237 The Red Fort at Delhi - so named because of the color of the sandstone used to build it - was designed to be a majestic symbol of the Moguls' power during their golden age, and it became the military and administrative center of the empire.

236 bottom Though still in use today, the Red Fort is no longer the heart of city life, when it was the site of slow parades of elephants and processions of troops in colorful uniforms.

the inlaid marble balcony overlooking an immense square used for public audiences, the square was completely covered by silk draperies, whereas the empire's nobility would sit in the hall, which would be clad in silver and gold. The private apartments, cooled and embellished by a number of gardens and fountains, were on the other side of the square.

The heart of the Red Fort – and of the Mogul Empire – was the Hall of Private Audience, with a ceiling made of solid silver supported by 32 columns encrusted with precious stones. Set in the middle was the dazzling Peacock Throne, the costliest chair ever made. It was literally covered with sapphires, rubies, diamonds, emeralds, and pearls. The throne was stolen and dismantled by Persian invaders in 1739. It was set on a marble slab, which the emperor had engraved with two zealous verses: "If there is a paradise on earth / it is here, it is here, oh, it is here!" Even the smaller rooms had silver ceilings, with the exception of the largest harem room: part of its ceiling was made of gold (it weighed 2.2 tons), and its walls were adorned with miniatures framed by 20,000 gems. In the gardens – only red flowers grew in one, while only white ones were raised in another – the fountains spewed rosewater. All the rooms had running water. The god of that paradise went to bed at exactly 10 p.m., as a lector hidden behind a screen read the emperor some of his favorite books until he fell asleep. The emperor enjoyed his lavish creation as an absolute monarch until 1658, and then for another eight years as a prisoner isolated from the world after he was deposed by his ungrateful son, Aurangzeb. (G.G.)

237 top The Mogul gardens - as geometric as Italian ones - had countless ponds and fountains, in keeping with Islamic tradition, as well as kiosks and pavilions where banquets were held.

237 bottom The Moti Masjid or Pearl Mosque, made entirely of white marble, and crowned by three large pear-shaped domes and slender minarets, was built by Aurangzeb in 1662. It is considered a masterpiece of Mogul architecture.

The Red Fort, Delhi

The Red Fort or Lal Qila was named after the structure's enormous red sandstone walls, and it is the capital's most famous monument.

It was built on the banks of the Jumna River as a citadel and imperial residence of the seventh Delhi (now Old Delhi).

Construction was completed in 1648 and required the best Indian craftsmen and incalculable sums of money. Despite its enormous moat and walls – still standing – that extend for over a mile, rising to a height of nearly 65 feet on the river side and nearly 100 on the city side, the fort was chiefly a symbol of power.

While the 100-foot-tall entrance portal astonishes visitors even today, the fort was by no means impregnable. In fact, the rooms on the river side were so exposed that they were easy targets for cannon fire.

The complex boasts public and private audience halls, marble palaces, an immense mosque, and splendid gardens. The portal of the Naubat-khana, above which was the musicians' gallery, led to the Diwan-i-Khas, where the council of state was held. (G.R.)

238 top and 239 top Most of the rooms and corridors at the Red Fort feature inlaid decorations with floral motifs, reflecting a style common to Persian and Turkish art of this period.

238-239 The Nahar-e-Bishisht, or Stream of Paradise, runs through the private apartments. It supplied water to the marble fountain carved in the shape of a lotus blossom and encrusted with gemstones.

239 Corridors with inlaid ceilings and elegant arches supported by enormous pillars lead to the Diwan-i-Khas, the Hall of Private Audience where the emperor held his councils of state and received ambassadors.

240-241 *The Diwan-i-Am, or Hall of Public Audience, is an enormous area with columns and cusped arches. The imperial throne is in the middle of the hall, under a marble baldachin. The chair of the Grand Vizier, the emperor's highest-ranking minister, also made of marble, is set in front of the throne.*

The Red Fort, Delhi

240 bottom In the Diwan-i-Am, the elevated platform holding the throne is decorated with an exquisite bas-relief of plants entwined to form geometric motifs.

241 top The Mahal-i-Khas, or Private Palace, was composed of three pavilions, clad with marble and inlaid with precious stones, or clad in precious metal. They were built between 1639 and 1649.

241 bottom Different bird species, created using precious stones, decorate one of the walls next to the throne in the Diwan-i-Am. This work has been attributed to the French artist Austin de Bordeaux, one of the many Europeans hired by the Mogul emperors.

Meherangarh, Jodhpur

INDIA

242-243 *The fortress at Jodhpur, dotted with balconies, galleries, and loggias, looks like a red sandstone sculpture. The sole access to the stronghold is via a narrow and tortuous path with a series of fortified bridges.*

242 bottom *"A Palace that might have been built by Titans and colored by the morning sun": this is how Kipling described Meherangarh, extravagantly laid out around a series of connected courtyards.*

243 *Set on a rocky 400-foot-high slope, Meherangarh towers over the landscape. The view from this vantage point extends for miles.*

The Rathor, the powerful clan that ruled over part of central India as early as 1,500 years ago, claimed to descend from Rama, hero of the Hindu epic poem *Ramayana*, and through him from the sun god Surya. The Muslim invasion forced them to seek refuge in the deserts of Rajasthan, where they founded the kingdom of Marwar. In 1459, this kingdom established its new capital at Jodhpur. The *rao* (ruler) Jodha was the one who chose that place on the eastern edge of the arid sands of the Thar, dominated by a rocky hill with a view that extended for miles. However, a hermit lived in the very cliffs where Jodha wanted to build the impressive acropolis of Meherangarh ("Majestic Fort"), and the *rao* was forced to drive him out.

The vengeful holy man cast a terrible curse on the ruler and his descendants. Every year famine would strike their kingdom, which already bore a fateful name: Marwar means "land of death." This indeed came to pass, and Jodha's prayers to the terrible hermit could only alleviate the curse but did not get rid of it. Consequently, there were famines every three or four years.

The construction of Meherangarh was completed in ten years thanks to the labor of 10,000 slaves and 500 elephants. The stones that had to be lifted were so heavy that the cords used to hoist them often caught fire in the pulleys. Its construction also claimed another life: that of its architect, who was immolated – willingly – to prevent him from building a similar marvel. The immolation sacrifice was attended by the ruler, his wives, their 17 sons and 52 daughters, as well as the architect's wife and children, who were granted an enormous piece of land in compensation. Over the centuries, the fortress was the site of many other sacrifices that, unfortunately, were less legendary: the ritual suicides (*sati*) of princesses who would throw themselves on the funeral pyre after the death of their husband, the king. To commemorate their gesture for posterity, as they went through the seventh gate of the palace they would henna their right hand to leave an imprint on the wall.

244-245 *Jali, lattice windows made of carved stone, are distinctive of Rajasthan's architecture. Their infinite decorative variations were inspired by the imagination of the artists or the whims of their clients.*

244 bottom left *The decorations in the residential sections are so intricate and lavish that these works are effectively stone embroidery and not mere sculptures.*

Meherangarh, Jodhpur

Though the British, who had already colonized India and had banned this horrible custom as early as 1829, in 1843, the six widows of the deceased ruler Man Singh died for their lord; some of them were just 15 years old. The last *sati* (human sacrifice) at Meherangarh took place in 1952 with the suicide of the wife of General Jahar Singh, governor of the palace. The funeral pyre was surrounded by an enormous crowd – virtually the entire population of the city – chanting Vedic hymns. Everyone knew what was happening, but the papers reported that "the police arrived too late." In the Hindu tradition, however, there could be no more glorious death for a *rani*. Sati was the name of the consort of the god Shiva, who entered the fire first to honor her husband. (G.G.))

245 top The rows of the slender columns on the three upper floors of this wing of the palace are interrupted by balconies that seem to be set on top of each other.

*245 bottom
Various galleries and balconies face the exterior, but many also overlook the numerous courtyards, which are enclosed by colonnades.*

244 bottom right Courtyards of different sizes, located between the buildings, are connected by galleries and elegantly sculpted doorways.

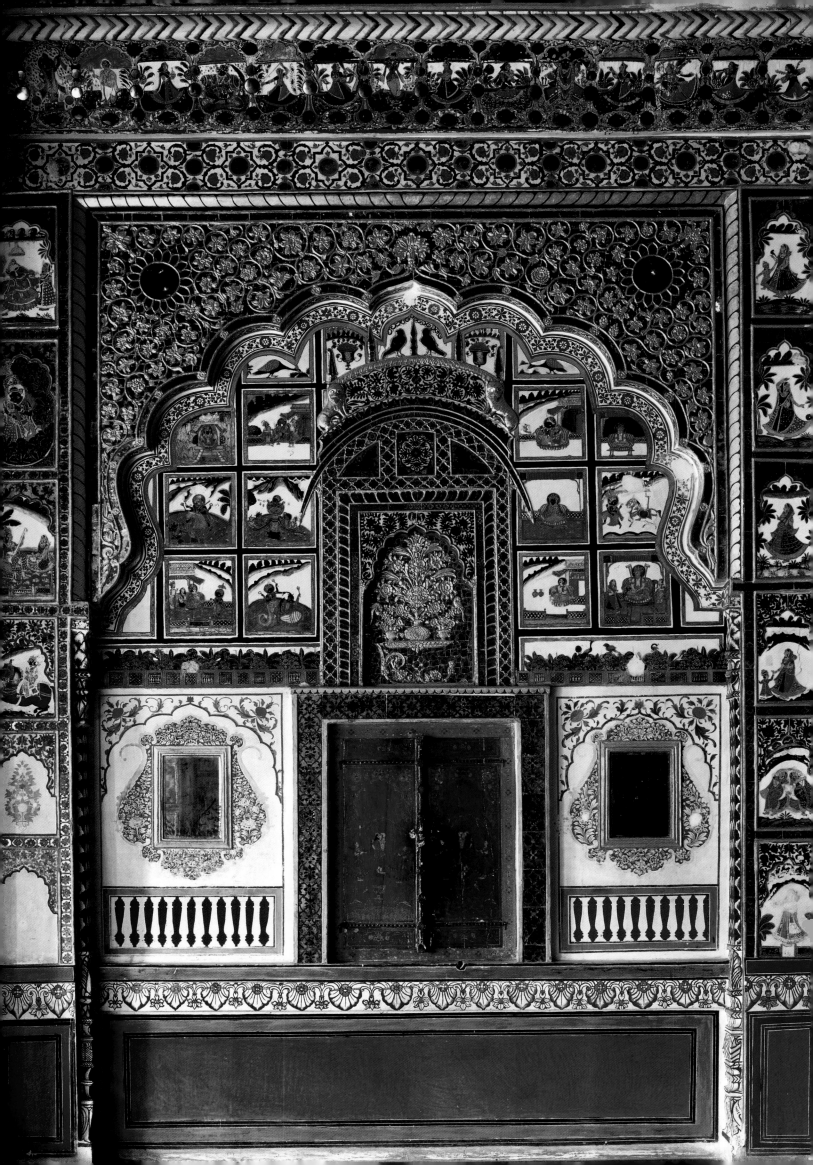

Meherangarh, Jodhpur

246 The lacquered walls of the enormous royal bedchamber at the Takhat Vilas are decorated with figures of dancing girls and tales of mythical lovers.

247 top Visitors' movements are playfully reflected by the mosaic mirror, framed by rows of dancers, set in the middle of the octagonal dome of one of the rooms at the Takhat Vilas.

247 center During the 1930s, someone decided to hang glass Christmas ornaments from the ceiling of this room at the Takhat Vilas. Nevertheless, these decorations go perfectly with the room's extravaganza of lights and colors.

247 bottom Jodhpur was the location of a famous painting school, which exported miniatures throughout the Indian subcontinent. Local artists painted the rooms of the Takhat Vilas as well as other residential areas at Meherangarh.

Meherangarh, Jodhpur

While Mogul palaces are paeans to symmetry, the residences of the Rajputs are fortified citadels and masterpieces of the ornate. The Meherangarh is accessed via a winding paved road that goes through seven massive fortified gates. The most beautiful are the Gate of Victory, the Gate of Triumph, the Iron Gate (the handprints of the maharajah's widows who immolated themselves on the pyre in 1843 can be seen near its wall), and the Gate of the Sun. The innermost part is composed of lavish palaces decorated with *jali*, lattice windows through which women could observe the life of the court. The rooms in these palaces now house the rich collections of Rajput weapons, miniatures, and carved doors of the Meherangarh Museum. The throne room, with a painted glass and gold ceiling, and triple bands of niches, is located in the Pearl Palace. North of the fort is the cenotaph of Maharajah Jaswant Singh II, who died in 1895. It has been compared to the Taj Mahal, but in place of the solemn lines distinctive of Mogul art, this monument is completely covered with intricate Rajput decorations. (G.R.)

248-249 *The Shesh Mahal, or Mirror Palace, dazzles visitors with its large mirror panels set in a lattice of little colored glass tiles, colorful Christmas ornaments, and murals.*

249 left *The Phool Mahal, or Flower Palace, was built in the 1700s as the private audience hall of the ruler, whose throne, covered by an umbrella, is visible in the background.*

249 top right *The Zenana, where the queen lived, was the most private and sacrosanct part of the palace. Like the rest of the palace, the women's apartments were also sumptuously decorated.*

249 bottom right *Seventy pounds of gold were used to gild the ceiling of the Moti Mahal, the Pearl Palace, which was originally built as a public audience hall. Hundreds of mirrors glitter amid the gilded decorations.*

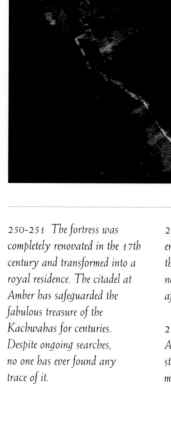

Jaigarh
Fort, Jaipur

INDIA

Jaigarh Fort – the "Victory Fort" at Amber Palace, the capital of the Kachwaha Rajputs in Jaipur, Rajasthan – was already 600 years old when Raja Man Singh began renovating it in 1600 to turn it into a magnificent residence. This work was completed by his grandson Jai Singh I, who was referred to as Mirza Raja, or "Noble Sovereign." The Indian emperors gave the Kachwahas, who were the Moguls' allies and relatives, the command of numerous armies and the governorships of various provinces. As a result, the Kachwahas would return to Jaigarh from their military campaigns and administrative posts laden with booty. These treasures would then be stashed in the deepest recesses of the fort, where they were safeguarded by the fierce warriors of the Mina tribe.

Whenever a new Kachwaha ruler rose to the throne, a Mina would blindfold him and lead him to the treasury. He would be allowed to choose only one item, and then no one else could enter the underground vault until a successor was crowned as the new ruler. The loyal Mina guards and the thick walls of Jaigarh were not enough to defend this fabulous treasure, however, so the city was surrounded by extensive walls and the surrounding hillsides were dotted with guard towers. When Emperor Aurangzeb asked Jai Singh II how Jaigarh was laid out, the Kachwaha ruler split open a pomegranate and, smiling, handed it to the emperor. The Kachwahas also boasted India's most powerful artillery, and what is still the world's largest cannon on wheels. Cast at Jaigarh's foundry, it is 8.2 feet tall, nearly 20 feet long, and weighs 55 tons. It took four elephants to drag it, and on the rare occasions when it was fired, its cannon shot was so powerful that it drove the water from the wells nearby: a minor ballistic earthquake.

250-251 The fortress was completely renovated in the 17th century and transformed into a royal residence. The citadel at Amber has safeguarded the fabulous treasure of the Kachwahas for centuries. Despite ongoing searches, no one has ever found any trace of it.

251 bottom The internal gardens, enclosed by the residential part of the stronghold and watered by a network of canals, were modeled after Mogul gardens.

252-253 The impressive fortress at Amber, with its lofty walls, is starkly outlined against the bare mountains.

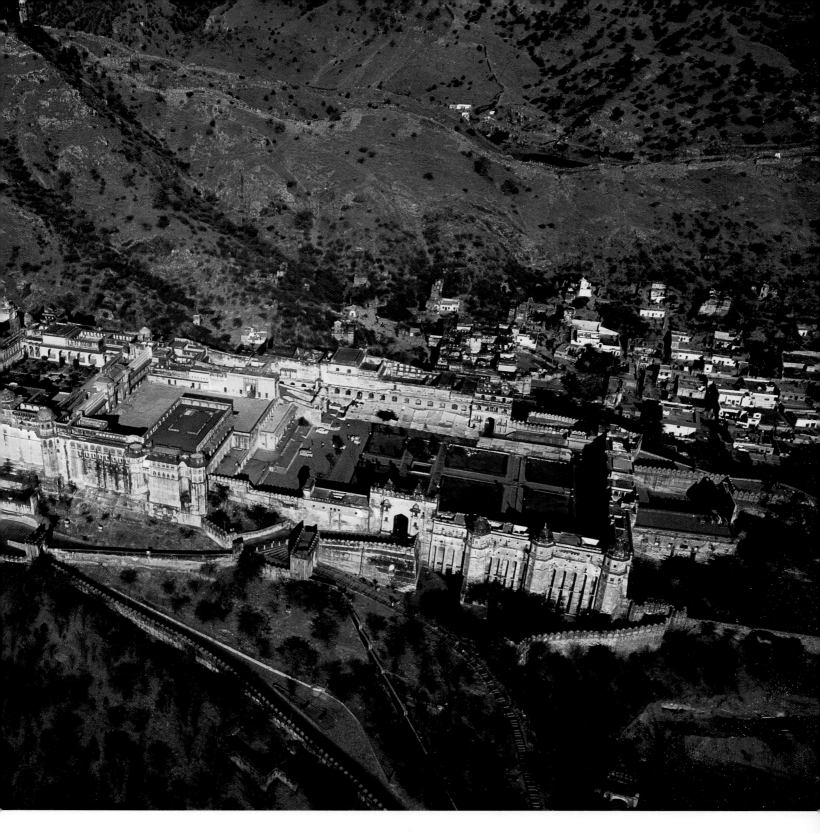

254-255 *The women from the royal family could look through the exquisitely carved lattice windows of the Ganesha Pol to observe - unseen - the ceremonies held in the Diwan-i-Am, or Hall of Public Audiences.*

Jaigarh Fort, Jaipur

Nevertheless, the ultimate defense of the stronghold and its treasures was entrusted to the heavenly powers. Man Singh, who had been governor of Bengal, brought the cult of Kali back from that faraway province. Kali was the goddess of death and destruction, and the *raja* built a temple to her inside the fort. Until only recently, goats and buffalos continued to be sacrificed to the goddess. Amber's wealth and beauty sparked the envy of suspicious Mogul rulers, fueled by the whispers of their zealous courtiers about these overly powerful vassals. As a result, in 1620 Emperor Jashangir decided that he would go and see the residence of that minor ruler who dared to compete with him in grandeur. After all, he considered Fatehpur Sikri, founded by his father Akbar in 1571, the most beautiful city in the world. Alerted about this illustrious and fearful visit, Jai Singh I chose prudence over ostentation, and had the walls of all the palaces covered with white plaster to hide their lavish decorations. Upon his arrival, the emperor was delighted to find a series of ordinary white buildings.

In 1970 – three and a half centuries later – the Indian government was also mocked by the Kachwahas' foresight. Enormous amounts of money were invested to start excavations to search for the fabulous treasure, said to be worth over $30 million. Not one thing was found. (G.G.)

254 bottom Decorated with frescoes and mosaics, the Ganesha Pol - the gate of the god Ganesha - led to the private apartments, which were separate from the rest of the fortress and had lovely internal gardens.

255 bottom Kiosks and pavilions, supported by delicate slender columns and protected by graceful domes, dot the immense and stately area around the building.

256-257 and 257 top The wings
of the enormous palace
at Amber are connected
by lovely colonnaded galleries,
decorated mainly with valuable
polychrome marble.

256 bottom and 257 bottom
The rooms inside the Ganesha Pol
are decorated with frescoes typical
of Rajput art, with the haunting
repetition of stylized plants and
flowers.

Jaigarh Fort, Jaipur

The *rajas* built Jaigarh Fort in the Rajput palatial style, ambitiously emulating the great Mogul residences. The walls were built of red sandstone, whereas prized marble was used for the interior. The palace itself, along with the royal apartments, is beyond the fortifications and is accessed via a cleverly devised grand avenue through splendid portals, halls, pavilions, temples, and shrines (one of which is dedicated to the goddess Kali, with immense silver portals), monumental staircases, and smaller palaces. The most well-known sections are the traditional public audience hall and the Shesh Mahal or Mirror Palace, with loggias, pavilions, terraces, and impressive and exquisitely crafted mirrors.

All the walls and pillars in the complex are decorated with intricate geometric or zoomorphic motifs and – naturally – there are frescoes of elephants, reflecting typical Hindu *horror vacui*. The women's apartments, set around a lovely courtyard and covered with brightly colored paintings, are intriguing. (G.R.)

258-259 Maota Lake, at the foot of the cliff where the fortress was built, was the main source of water, which was channeled through a complex plumbing system that even went to the upper floors.

Himeji

JAPAN

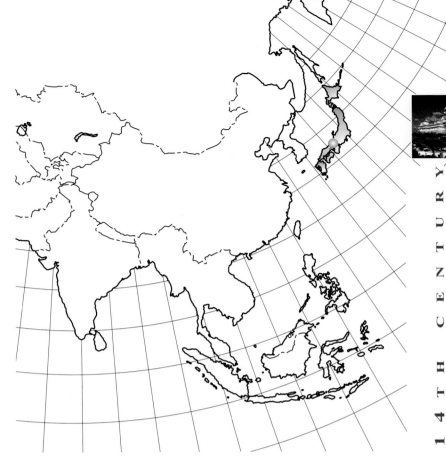

The white castle of Himeji stands out starkly against the dark pine forests that endeared Harima Province to the poets, writers, and painters of ancient Japan. Perched on a crag overlooking the town that developed around it, the castle was referred to as Shirasagi-jo, "White Heron Castle," due to its contrast with the black castle of Okayama, known as U-jo, or the "Crow Castle." Construction began in 1346, during a period of extraordinarily complicated and unending wars in which everyone was fighting against everyone else.

The Akamatsu, the first lords of the castle, lost the stronghold to the Ashikaga. Considered the "Medici of Japan" because of their role as patrons of the arts and literature, the Ashikaga ruled the archipelago from their residence in Kyoto, where they had installed an illegitimate dynasty while the legitimate emperors roamed the southern islands in poverty. As the spread of Buddhism began to curb the traditions of the Samurai, paintings, lacquered works, porcelain, bronze artifacts, and silk were brought into the White Heron Castle alongside swords, bows, banners, and armor.

In 1467, the descendants of the Akamatsu regained control of the castle, which they maintained until 1577, when Oda Nobunaga formed a coalition of large landowners and ousted the Ashikaga. As a reward, Nobunaga assigned the castle to his general, Toyotomi Hideyoshi, who updated the structure and added 30 small towers. Though of very lowly origins (he started out as Nobunaga's groom), Hideyoshi managed to bring peace to the troubled empire. He was adopted by the noble Fujiwara family and became prime minister. He also reorganized the army, outfitting it with cannons and harquebuses, which Portuguese merchants had introduced to Japan, and attempted to invade Korea.

When Hideyoshi died in 1598, Himeji was given to Ikeda Terumasa as a fief in 1601 to reward him for his courage during the Battle of Sekigahara, which gave control of Japan to another great statesman and warlord, Ieyasu Tokugawa. Tokugawa's descendants ruled the empire until 1868. This marked the beginning of a period of economic prosperity and good administration. As a result, Terumasa's work to fortify Himeji – it had 50 towers at this point – proved to be useless. The castle was never attacked again, and the only time it was used for military purposes was when it housed the command post of a Japanese army division from the late 19th century until 1931, when it was proclaimed a national treasure. (G.G.)

260 Himeji was dubbed the "White Heron Castle" because of its white walls. The floors, built in a step-like arrangement, are accentuated by gracefully curved roofs. This structure is typical of Japanese feudal castles.

261 Himeji and Osakajo, the stronghold near Osaka, are the best-preserved castles in Japan. Himeji's snow-white buildings with gray roofs dominate the countryside of Harima Province.

This is the only castle in the "Land of the Gods" that, from an architectural standpoint, represents Japanese culture as a whole. Indeed, it has maintained the purity of the lines of the "Japanese Renaissance." The castle was built in three phases. In 1346, when it belonged to Sadanori Akamatsu, it had no outside walls and, as such, resembled a Norman *motte*. In 1580, when the famous general Toyotomi Hideyoshi enlarged it and the Portuguese introduced firearms, completely changing the art of fortification, wide moats and thick walls were added. Moreover, its layout was altered to allow infantrymen armed with muskets to move about quickly.

The third remodeling was carried out by General Terumasa Ikeda in the 17th century. This work took nine years to complete and employed 50,000 laborers, who were divided into teams that competed against each other. The teams were assigned to build different portions of the castle and they were led by a hierarchical structure of ingenious master carpenters. The finest stone and lumber were used. The castle covered an area of nearly 570 acres, with a spiral layout forming a veritable labyrinth. Engelbert Kaempfer (1651-1716), a physician with the Dutch East India Company, stated that he had never seen anything like it in Europe. The castle had a main tower that was 100 feet tall (*Daitenshukaku*), three small towers (*Shotenshukaku*) and a donjon (*Tenshukaku*). Its enormous warehouses were used to store rice and weapons. Its walls were built with a progressively larger curvature – increasing from 30° to 40° – to support the colossal weight of the *Daitenshukaku* and prevent possible earthquake damage. Two enormous 79-foot pillars served as the bearing structure of the tower. Seen from the outside, the tower looked as if it were divided into five floors but there were actually seven, a stratagem designed to confuse the enemy. The castle has 80 main gates, numerous secret passages, temples, a completely separate administrative compound, and stables. The fine art of stonecutting is reflected in the principle of *Nedori no Gumen*, "the art of laying the foundations of a rampart." (G.R.)

262 bottom Massive wooden beams sustain the various floors of the edifice, built to withstand the earthquakes that often hit the Japanese islands.

262-263 The elegant complexity of the façade is offset by the utter simplicity of the interior, a feature distinctive of all Japanese dwellings.

Himeji

263 bottom *White walls decorated with red lacquered beams characterize the rooms and halls of the lower part of Himeji Castle.*

264-265 Château Frontenac is located in the heart of Quebec. Its main tower is enclosed by external walls, imitating France's Renaissance chateaux.

264 bottom With its latest additions, the hotel now has 618 rooms and 24 suites. It has become the emblem of the Canadian city and its most distinctive urban element.

Château Frontenac

CANADA

Château Frontenac was built in 1893 in the heart of old Quebec, in a style that the guidebooks of the *Belle Epoque* referred to as "French baronial" but may actually be defined as a hybrid. Now one of the most famous and impressive hotels in the world, it was built as a symbol of the power and prestige of William Van Horne, president of the Canadian Pacific Railway built across Canada to link the Atlantic and the Pacific. The immense edifice was subsequently enlarged in 1897-99, in 1926, and then again in 1992. The tower, which is the building's most distinctive feature, was built between 1920 and 1924. It was built over an area that was originally occupied by an actual stronghold, Fort St. Louis, built in 1620 by Samuel de Champlain, the founder of Quebec. The original fort was destroyed during a fire in 1834. One of its stones, bearing the Maltese Cross, was found among the ruins and was embedded in the wall under the entrance of Château Frontenac. The castle was named after Louis de Buade, Count of Frontenac, who was the governor of New France – the French colony of Canada – from 1672 to 1698.

Since the day it opened, Château Frontenac has hosted illustrious guests, from Charles Lindbergh to Alfred Hitchcock, King George VI of Great Britain, and Chiang Kai-shek. The Quebec Conference, held here in 1943 between British Prime Minister Winston Churchill and American President Franklin D. Roosevelt, was decisive for the outcome of World War II. (G.G.)

Acknowledged as a Gallic symbol on the American continent, Château Frontenac it was designed by architect Bruce Price, who also designed Montreal's Windsor Station. Price studied a number of medieval and Renaissance buildings, modeling the castle after French 15th-century châteaux. When the hotel opened, it had 170 rooms and three suites, but today it boasts 618 rooms and 24 suites. The notable additions to the hotel were the work of Walter S. Painter (Mont-Carmel Wing) and of Edward and William Maxwell (Saint-Louis and Riverview Wings). The enchantment of color is always fundamental in architecture: brick was used to clad the construction, but Saint-Marc-des-Carrières limestone was used for the ground floor and all the ornamentation work. The only exception is the side where the Governors' Garden is located. Here the architects used Dolomitic limestone known as Chazy, from Saint-François-de-Sales on Ile Jésus, which has a distinctive yellowish-brown hue. Inside, the walls on the ground floor are finished in French Rippe Doré marble. Pink Villarville marble was used for the flooring. (G.R.).

265 Dormers, spires, towers, and mansards: the entire architectural repertory of authentic French chateaux has been lavished on this false cousin across the Atlantic.

Castillo de San Marcos

USA

266-267 *San Marcos, which has a square layout and is fortified by four mighty bastions, is a typical example of the fortresses built by the Spanish in its American possessions. Though simple in structure, they were designed to withstand extended sieges.*

267 top *This 17th-century drawing shows a plan of San Marcos, indicating how the artillery was arranged in the fortress and depicting several wooden constructions that no longer exist.*

Though the Spanish were familiar with Florida as early as the turn of the 16th century, they did not settle there until much later. In 1565, Pedro Menéndez de Avilés landed at Matanzas Bay and built the *presidio* of St. Augustine to protect the Bahamas Channel. The Spanish fleet used this sea route every year to return to Spain with bars of silver produced in Mexico and Peru. As a result, their ships were often attacked by the pirates who dominated the Caribbean and by the corsairs of powers hostile to Spain, France, and above all, England. After buccaneers attacked St. Augustine in 1668, the Spanish decided to replace the original wooden structure with a stone fortress. Construction began in 1672 and the stronghold was named Castillo de San Marcos.

Queen Anne's War, also known as the War of the Spanish Succession, broke out 30 years later, and San Marcos faced its first attack by the English based in the Carolinas. However, the British ships were trapped in the bay of St. Augustine by a rescue fleet from Havana. Not only did the British have to retreat, but they were forced to burn their ships to keep them

267 bottom San Marcos controlled the Bahamas Channel. This passage was vital for the Spanish fleet, which used this route to transport loads of Mexican and Peruvian silver back to Spain.

from being seized by the Spaniards. Following this attack, the fortress was enlarged and fortified, and walls were built around the city. In 1738, the British established a blockade and bombarded the stronghold, but once again they were forced to retreat after a 38-day siege. The Britiish did not take over the city until 1763, following the Treaty of Paris attributing Florida to Great Britain.

The city became important to the Crown and following the outbreak of the American Revolution, St. Augustine remained loyal to King George III. As a result, the fort was used as a base to fight the Spanish forces allied with the rebels. When America finally gained its independence, Florida was returned to Spain in 1784. The Spanish held it until 1821, when it was ceded to the United States. The fortress was remodeled and renamed Fort Marion. During the Civil War the Confederates held the fortress, but the Union forces captured it without firing a single shot. It was converted into an army prison, and was finally declared a national monument in 1900. (G.G.)

San Marcos is a square with ramparts at its four corners. Its extensive layout is reminiscent of several European and, in particular Italian counterparts, notably the fortress at L'Aquila in Abruzzo. Tellingly, the architects of both of these strongholds were Spanish. The fortress was designed in keeping with the principles of bastioned defense, resulting in an extremely compact shape and buttressed ramparts. The structure foreshadowed that of the 19th-century fortress and it was built to ensure strategic control over the area. The walls were built using a local stone referred to as *coquina* by the Spanish. The term means "little shell" and, in fact, *coquina* was composed of fossilized shell deposits that had bonded to form stone, which was quarried in Havana and transported to Florida. Mortar was made by baking a mixture of oyster shell and sand in kilns. It took 23 years to complete the stronghold, which was encircled by a moat and equipped with cannons. Its perimeter is over half a mile long, its walls 30 feet tall, and about 10 feet thick. The moat is nearly 40 feet wide. The interior is divided into approximately 20 sleeping quarters. The fortress is now part of a national park. (G.R.)

INDEX

PHOTOGRAPHIC CREDITS

page1 Jason Hawkes/Corbis/Contrasto
pages 2-3 Guido Alberto Rossi/The image Bank
pages 4-5 Giovanni Simeone/Sime/Sie
page 6 Jason Hawkes
pages 12-13 Temi Editrice
pages 14-15 Marcello Bertinetti/Archivio White Star
page 16 top Angelo Colombo/Archivio White Star
page 16 bottom Giovanni Simeone/Sime/Sie
pages 16-17 Massimo Ripani/Sime/Sie
page 17 Massimo Ripani/Sime/Sie
page 18 Giovanni Simeone/Sime/Sie
pages 18-19 Giovanni Simeone/Sime/Sie
page 19 top Angelo Colombo/Archivio White Star
page 19 center Giulio Veggi/Archivio White Star
page 20 Aisa
page 21 top Erich Lessing/Contrasto
page 21 bottom Zanettini/Laif/Contrasto
page 22 top Bridgeman Art Library/Archivio Alinari
page 22 center Bruce Yuan-Yue Bi/Lonely Planet Images
page 22 bottom Photoservice/AKG
pages 22-23 Sandro Vannini/Corbis/Contrasto
page 23 Sandro Vannini/Corbis/Contrasto
page 24 top left Angelo Colombo/Archivio White Star
page 24 top right Felipe J. Alcoceba
page 24 bottom Antonio Real Hurtado
pages 24-25 Daniel Phelippe
page 25 ICP
page 26 Antonio Real Hurtado
page 27 top left Felipe J. Alcoceba
page 27 topright Angelo Colombo/Archivio White Star
page 27 center and bottom Antonio Real Hurtado
page 28 top Angelo Colombo/Archivio White Star
page 28 center Wojtek Buss
pages 28-29 Wojtek Buss
page 29 Wojtek Buss
page 30 Torcuato Fandila
pages 30-31 David Barnes/Danita Delimont
page 31 Wojtek Buss
page 32 left Felipe J. Alcoceba
page 32 right Angelo Colombo/Archivio White Star
pages 32-33 Aisa
page 33 left Bridgeman Art Library/Archivio Alinari
page 33 right Felipe J. Alcoceba
page 34 top Aisa
page 34 center Aisa
page 34 bottom Guido Cozzi/Atlantide Phototravel
pages 34-35 Guido Cozzi/Atlantide Phototravel
page 36 Aisa
page 37 top Aisa
page 37 bottom Felipe J. Alcoceba
pages 38-39 G.V.P./Agefotostock/Contrasto
page 40 Bibliotheque Nationale de Fance
pages 40-41 Archivio PUBBLI AER FOTO
page 41 top Angelo Colombo/Archivio White Star
page 41 center Diana Mayfield/Lonely Planet Images
page 41 bottom Erich Lessing/Contrasto
page 42 Giovanni Dagli Orti/Chateau de Blois/The Art Archive
pages 42-43 Eisermann/Laif/Contrasto
page 43 top Giovanni Dagli Orti/The Art Archive
page 43 center Giovanni Dagli Orti/The Art Archive
page 43 bottom Alamy Images
page 44 Giovanni Dagli Orti/Chateau de Blois/The Art Archive
pages 44-45 Giovanni Dagli Orti/The Art Archive
page 45 Alamy Images
page 46 Bridgeman Art Library/Archivio Alinari
pages 46-47 Alamy Images
page 47 top left Angelo Colombo/Archivio White Star
page 47 top right Bridgeman Art Library/Archivio Alinari
page 47 bottom Gérard Blot/Photo RMN
pages 48-49 Michelle Garrett/Corbis/Contrasto
page 49 Sandro Vannini/Corbis/Contrasto
page 50 top Sandro Vannini/Corbis/Contrasto
page 50 bottom Giovanni Dagli Orti/Chateau de Chambord/The Art Archive
pages 50-51 Bertrand GardelHemisphers Images
page 50 Sandro Vannini/Corbis/Contrasto
page 52 left and right Giovanni Dagli Orti
pages 52-53 Giovanni Dagli Orti
page 53 Giovanni Dagli Orti
page 54 left Olimpo Fantuz/Sime/Sie
page 54 right Angelo Colombo/Archivio White Star
pages 54-55 Manfred Linke/Laif-Rea/Contrasto
page 55 Olimpo Fantuz/Sime/Sie
pages 56-57 Olimpo Fantuz/Sime/Sie
page 58 left and right Giovanni Dagli Orti/The Art Archive
pages 58-59 Giovanni Dagli Orti/The Art Archive
page 59 top Bridgeman Art Library/Archivio Alinari
page 59 bottom Giovanni Dagli Orti/The Art Archive
page 60 Giovanni Dagli Orti/The Art Archive
page 61 Giovanni Dagli Orti/The Art Archive
page 62 top left Angelo Colombo/Archivio White Star
page 62 top right Bridgeman Art Library/Archivio Alinari
page 62 bottom Royalty-Free/Corbis/Contrasto
pages 62-63 John Frumm/Hemispheres Images
page 63 John Frumm/Hemispheres Images
page 64 Giovanni Dagli Orti/The Art Archive
pages 64-65 John Frumm/Hemispheres Images
page 65 top Giovanni Dagli Orti/The Art Archive
page 65 bottom Giovanni Dagli Orti/The Art Archive
page 66 Bertrand Gardel/Hemispheres Images
pages 66-67 Jb Rabouan/Imagefrance.com/Hemispheres Images
page 67 top Angelo Colombo/Archivio White Star
page 67 bottom Alamy Images
pages 68-69 John Elk III/Lonely Planet Images
page 69 top Alamy Images
page 69 bottom David Barnes/Agefotostock/Contrasto
page 70 Hans Wiesenhofer/Anzenberger/Contrasto
pages 70-71 Bruno Barbier/Hemispheres Images
page 71 top Hans Wiesenhofer/Anzenberger/Contrasto
page 71 center Alamy Images
page 72 Angelo Colombo/Archivio White Star
pages 72-73 Guillaume Team
page 73 Aisa
page 74 top Bertrand Riege/Hemispheres Images
page 74 bottom Guillaume Team
pages 74-75 Guillaume Team
page 75 Guillaume Team
pages 76-77 Daniel Philippe
page 77 Angelo Colombo/Archivio White Star
page 78 Centre des monuments nationaux, Paris
pages 78-79 Massimo Ripani/Sime/Sie
page 80 top left Livio Bourbon/Archivio White Star
page 80 top right Angelo Colombo/Archivio White Star
page 80 bottom Livio Bourbon/Archivio White Star
pages 80-81 Antonio Attini/Archivio White Star
page 81 Livio Bourbon/Archivio White Star
page 82 top, center and bottom Livio Bourbon/Archivio White Star
page 83 Ashford Castle
page 84 Jason Hawkes
page 85 top left Lowell Georgia/Corbis/Contrasto
page 85 top right Angelo Colombo/Archivio White Star
page 85 bottom Historical Picture Archive/Corbis/Contrasto
page 86 Krinitz/Laif/Contrasto
pages 86-87 Steve Vider/Sime/Sie
page 87 top ICP
page 87 bottom Historic Scotland
page 88 top Angelo Colombo/Archivio White Star
page 88 bottom ICP
pages 88-89 ICP
page 89 Massimo Borchi/Archivio White Star
page 90 top Vittoriano Rastelli/Corbis/Contrasto
page 90 bottom Vittoriano Rastelli/Corbis/Contrasto
pages 90-91 Vittoriano Rastelli/Corbis/Contrasto
page 91 Massimo Borchi/Archivio White Star
page 92 The Photolibrary Wales
pages 92-93 Cardiff Councuil
page 93 top Angelo Colombo/Archivio White Star
page 93 center The Photolibrary Wales
page 93 bottom Patrick Frilet/Hemispheres Images
page 94 Cardiff Councuil
pages 94-95 The Photolibrary Wales
page 95 top The Photolibrary Wales
page 95 bottom Cardiff Councuil
page 96 top a sinitra Angelo Colombo/Archivio White Star
page 96 top right Giovanni Dagli Orti/Museé du Chateau de Versailles/The Art Archive
page 96 bottom ICP
pages 96-97 ICP
page 97 Photoservice Electa/AKG
page 98 top Ian Jones/FSP/Gamma/Contrasto
page 98 bottom Tim Graham/Corbis Sygma/Contrasto
pages 98-99 Ingolf Pompe/Hemispheres Images
page 99 Alamy Images
page 100 Bridgeman Art Library/Archivio Alinari
page 101 top Corbis Sygma/Contrasto
page 101 bottom left Corbis Sygma/Contrasto
page 101 bottom right Tim Graham/Corbis Sygma/Contrasto
page 102 top Tim Graham /Corbis Sygma/Contrasto
page 102 bottom Tim Graham /Corbis/Contrasto
pages 102-103 ICP
page 103 bottom left Tim Graham/Corbis/Contrasto
pages 103 bottom right Tim Graham/Corbis/Contrasto
page 104 top Angelo Colombo/Archivio White Star
page 104 center ICP
pages 104-105 Jason Hawkes
page 105 ICP
page 106 top Richard T. Nowiz/Corbis/Contrasto
page 106 bottom Alamy Images
pages 106-107 Warwick Castle
page 107 Alamy Images
page 108 top left Angelo Colombo/Archivio White Star

271

pages 226-227 Marcello Bertinetti/Archivio White Star
page 227 Giulio Veggi/Archivio White Star
page 228-229 Ivan Zupoic/Agefotostock/Marka
page 229 top left Elizabeta Habic/Postojnska jama, turizem Postojna
page 229 top right Angelo Colombo/Archivio White Star
page 229 bottom Elizabeta Habic/Postojnska jama, turizem Postojna
page 230 Srecko Sajn/Postojnska jama, turizem Postojna
pages 230-231 Toni Anzenberger/Anzenberger/Contrasto
page 231 Srecko Sajn/Postojnska jama, turizem Postojna
page 232 Sandro Vannini/Corbis/Contrasto
page 233 top left Hungarian National Tourist Office
page 233 top right Angelo Colombo/Archivio White Star
page 233 bottom Focus Team
page 234 Wojtek Buss
pages 234-235 Marka Collection
page 235 top Angelo Colombo/Archivio White Star
page 235 bottom David Else/Lonely Planet Images
page 236 Marcello Bertinetti/Archivio White Star
pages 236-237 Lindsay Hebberd/Corbis/Contrasto
page 237 top Angelo Colombo/Archivio White Star
page 237 center Craig Lowell/Corbis/Contrasto

page 237 bottom Francesco Venturi/Corbis/Contrasto
page 238 Francesco Venturi/Corbis/Contrasto
pages 238-239 Macduff Everton/Corbis/Contrasto
page 239 top Ross Pictures/Corbis/Contrasto
page 239 right Nicolas Sapieha/Corbis/Contrasto
page 240 Massimo Borchi/Archivio White Star
pages 240-241 Massimo Borchi/Archivio White Star
page 241 top and bottom Massimo Borchi/Archivio White Star
page 242 Thomas Dix
pages 242-243 Thomas Dix
page 243 top Angelo Colombo/Archivio White Star
page 243 center Nicolas Chorier/Gamma/Contrasto
page 244 left Thomas Dix
page 244 right Alamy Images
pages 244-245 Arvind Garg/Corbis/Contrasto
page 245 top Thomas Dix
page 245 bottom ICP
page 246 Thomas Dix
page 247 top, center and bottom Thomas Dix
page 248 Thomas Dix
page 249 top Thomas Dix
page 249 bottom left and right Thomas Dix
page 250 Angelo Colombo/Archivio White Star
pages 250-251 Yann Arthus-Bertrand/Corbis/Contrasto

page 251 Marcello Bertinetti/Archivio White Star
pages 252-253 Yann Arthus-Bertrand/Corbis/ Contrasto
page 254 Guido Cozzi/Atlantide Phototravel
pages 254-255 Riccardo Spila/Sime/Sie
page 255 Marcello Bertinetti/Archivio White Star
page 256 Marcello Bertinetti/Archivio White Star
pages 256-257 Guido Cozzi/Atlantide Phototravel
page 257 top and bottom Marcello Bertinetti/Archivio White Star
pages 258-259 Riccardo Spila/Sime/Sie
page 260 Steve Vidler/Sime/Sie
page 261 top Angelo Colombo/Archivio White Star
page 261 bottom Marcello Bertinetti/Archivio White Star
page 262 Archivio Iconografico, S.A./Corbis/Contrasto
pages 262-263 Michael S. Yamashita/Corbis/Contrasto
page 263 Craig Lowell
page 264 Philippe Renault/Hémisphères Images
pages 264-265 Yann Arthus-Bertrand/Corbis/Contrasto
page 265 top Angelo Colombo/Archivio White Star
page 265 bottom Alamy Images
pages 266-267 Jim Wark
page 267 top left Bettman/Corbis/Contrasto
page 267 top right Angelo Colombo/Archivio White Star
page 267 center Jim Wark

BIBLIOGRAPHY

Various authors, *Haut-Koenigsburg*, Paris 1996.
Various authors, *Il Libro d'Oro dei castelli della Loira*, Florence 1997.
Allen Brown, R., *English Medieval Castles*, London 1954.
Alvensleben, U. von, Koenigswald, H. von, *Schlösser und Schicksale. Herrensitze und Burgen zwischen Donau und Rhein*, Berlin 1970.
Anderson, W., *Castles of Europe*, New York 1984.
Anonymous, *Clisson. Visite au Château et à la Garenne*, Nantes 1885.
Lady Armstrong, *Bamburgh Castle: the home of Lord and Lady Armstrong and Family*, Norwich 1994.
Baroda, Maharajah of, *The Palaces of India*, London 1980.
Beltrami, L., *Il Castello di Milano*, Milan 1912.
Berthou, P. de, *Clisson et ses monuments*, Nantes 1910.
Borkowski, J., *Zamkik panstwa krzyzackiego*, Warsaw 1999.
Boson, G., *Il castello di Issogne*, Novara 1951.
Boson, G., *Le Château de Fénis*, Novara 1953.
Cruden, S., *The Scottish Castle*, Edinburgh 1960.
Dattilo, V., *Castel dell'Ovo fra storia e leggenda*, Naples 1956.
Desing, J., *The Royal Castle of Neuschwastein*, Lechbruck, 1998.
Dieulafoy, M., *L'arte in Spagna e Portogallo*, Bergamo, 1913.
Lady Elphinstone, *Glamis Castle*, Derby 1975.
Engel, H.U., *Burgen und Schlösser in Böhmen*, Frankfurt, 1961.
Giacosa, P., *Il castello di Issogne*, Verona 1968.
Gorfer, A., *Castel Beseno*, Rovereto, 1979.
Gotze, H., *Castel del Monte. Forma, simbologia, architettura*, Milan 1986.
Gradenigo, P., *Postumia*, Postojna 1935.

Gremaud, H., Chatton, E., *Le château de Gruyères*, Villars-sur-Glâne 1995.
Gyorgy, R., *Varosok; Varak; Kastelyok; regi magyarorszagi latkepek/Towns Castles Mansions; old Hungarian views; Stadte, burgen, schlösser; alte ungarische veduten*, Budapest 1995.
Holbach, M.M., *Dalmatia*, London 1908.
Innes-Smith, R., *Glamis Castle: seat of the Earl of Strathmore and Kinghorne*, Derby 1989.
Ionescu, G., *Istoria arhitecturii in România*, Bucharest 1963.
Iorga, *Les châteaux occidentaux en Roumanie*, Bucharest 1929.
Johansson, A., *The Castle of Kalmarsund*, Kalmar 1998.
Kinoshita, J., Palevsky, N., *Gateway to Japan*, Tokyo 1998.
Krizanova, E., *Slovak Castles, Manors and Châteaux*, Bratislava 1998.
Kubu, N., *Le château fort de Karlstejn*, Prague, 1996.
Lancmanis, I., *Schloss Rundale*, Rundale 2003.
Lancmanis, I., *Ernst Johann Biron 1690-1990. Katalog der Ausstellung im Schloss Rundale*, Rundale 1993.
Leash, H.G., *Irish Castles and Castellated Houses*, Dundalk, 1941.
Lise, G. (ed.), *Castelli e palazzi d'Italia*, Sancasciano 1982.
Livermore, H., *A History of Portugal*, Cambridge 1966.
Mehling, M., *Knaurs Kulturführer in Farbe Moskau*, Munich 1990.
Michel, F., *Burg Eltz*, Munich 1969.
Mierzwinski , M., *Malbork. The castle of the Teutonic knights*, Bydgoszcz 2001.
Naef, A., Schmid, O., *Album illustrant le guide official au Château de Chillon*, Vevey 1890.

Naef, A., *Château de Chillon*, Lausanne 1937.
Ortiz-Echagüe, J., *España: castillos y alcazares*, Madrid 1956.
Ottendorf-Simrock, W., *Castles on the Rhine*, Bonn 1972.
Piper, O., *Oesterreischische Burgen*, Vienna 1904.
Pons, M., *Bonaguil, château de rêve*, Saverdun 1966.
Raemy, D. de, *Grandson*, Bern 1987.
Ramée, D., *Monographie du château de Heidelberg*, Paris 1859.
Reicke, E., *Geschichte der Reichsstadt Nürnberg von dem ersten urkundlichen Nachweis ihres Bestehens bis zu ihrem Übergang an das Königreich Bayern (1806)*. Nuremberg 1896.
Sainz de Robles, F., *Castillos en España*, Madrid 1962.
Schlegel, R., *Festung Hohensalzburg*, Salzburg 1955.
Schick, A., *Furniture for the Dream King. Ludwig II and the Munich Court Cabinet-Maker Anton Pössenbacher*, Stuttgart 2003.
Slade, H.G., *Glamis Castle*, London 2000.
Steinbrecht, C., *Die Ordensburgen der Hochmeisterzeit in Preussen*, Berlin 1920.
Tabarelli, G.M., *Castelli, rocche e mura d'Italia*, Busto Arsizio 1983.
Tabarelli, G.M., *Castelli del Trentino*, Milan 1974.
Trcka, M., *Château de Hluboká*, Ceské Budejovice 2002.
Tillmann, C., *Lexicon der deutschen Burgen und Schlössen*, Stuttgart 1958-61.
Valvasor, J.W., *Die Ehre des Herzogthums Crain*, Laybach 1689.
Turnbull, S., Dennis, P., *Japanese Castles 1540-1640*, New York, 2003.
Willemsen, C.A., *Castel del Monte, die Krone Apuliens*, Wiesbaden 1955.
Wirth, Z., J. Benda, J., *Burgen und Schlösser (Böhmen und Mähren)*, Prague 1955.

ACKNOWLEDGMENTS

The publisher would like to thank:
Geneviève Parent, Public Relations Director, Fairmont Le Château (Frontenac, Quebec)
Mario Galli (Trieste, Italy); Johanna Ehrenberg-Wenger (Grandson, Switzerland);
Gunilla Ericcson (Stockolm, Sweden); Karin Aschberger (Spittal, Austria);
Chyla and Sobanski Families (Wroclaw, Poland); Pascale Olivaux (Montmeyran, France);
Raoul Blanchard, Gruyères Castle Curator (Gruyères, Switzerland);
Imants Lancmanis, Rundale Castle Director (Pilsrundale, Latvia);
Warwick Castle (Warwick, Great Britain)

METRO BOOKS
New York

An Imprint of Sterling Publishing
387 Park Avenue South
New York, NY 10016

METRO BOOKS and the distinctive Metro Books logo are trademarks of Sterling Publishing Co., Inc.

© 2005 by White Star Publishers
is a registered trademark property of De Agostini Libri S.p.A.

This 2013 edition published by Metro Books,
by arrangement with De Agostini Libri S.p.A.

ISBN 978-1-4351-4845-1

Library of Congress Cataloging-in-Publication Data

For information about custom editions, special sales, and premium and corporate purchases, please contact Sterling Special Sales at 800-805-5489 or specialsales@sterlingpublishing.com.

Manufactured in China

2 4 6 8 10 9 7 5 3 1

www.sterlingpublishing.com